GOOD MONEY

GOOD MONEY

A GUIDE
TO PROFITABLE
SOCIAL INVESTING
IN THE '90S
RITCHIE P. LOWRY

W · W · NORTON & COMPANY NEW YORK · LONDON

The text of this book
is composed in 11/13 Electra,
with the display set in
Gill Sans Extra Bold and Bold and Electra Cursive.
Composition and Manufacturing by
The Maple-Vail Book Manufacturing Group.
Book design and display art by
Margaret M. Wagner.

First published as a Norton paperback 1993

Library of Congress Cataloging-in-Publication Data
Lowry, Ritchie P., 1926–
Good money : a guide to profitable social investing in the '90s /
by Ritchie P. Lowry.
p.   cm.
Includes index.
1. Investments—Social aspects—United States—Handbooks, manuals,
etc.   2. Industry—Social aspects—United States—Handbooks,
manuals, etc.   3. Investments—United States—Moral and ethical
aspects—Handbooks, manuals, etc.   4. Success in business—United
States—Handbooks, manuals, etc.   I. Title.
HG4910.L68   1991
332.6'78'0973—dc20   90–46989

ISBN 0–393–30951-7

W. W. Norton & Company, Inc.
500 Fifth Avenue, New York, N.Y. 10110
W. W. Norton & Company Ltd.
10 Coptic Street, London WC1A 1PU

3 4 5 6 7 8 9 0

TO MY GRANDSONS—
JASON, ETHAN, AND COLIN
—IN THE HOPE THAT THEY
ARE GROWING UP
IN A MORE PEACEFUL AND
PROSPEROUS WORLD

CONTENTS

7

AN IDEA WHOSE TIME HAS COME

Walking through the Energy Investment Minefield
Environmentalism and SRI
Recognizing Corporate Flimflam
Animal Rights and SRI
Women and SRI
130

8

SRI INTERNATIONAL

Foreign Opportunities for Social Investors
How Foreign SRI Pays Off
Cautions for U.S. Investors Going Foreign
Foreign SRI Advisers
148

9

AND THE BEAT GOES ON

"Good Dows" Continue to Outperform Wall Street's Dows
More Opportunities for the Small Investor
Shareholder Action Increases and Becomes More Influential in 1991 and 1992
Environmentalism Takes Hold in the 90s
Tracking Corporate Social Behavior
SRI Spreads Globally
170

EPILOGUE

Can Capitalism Ever Be Ethical?
Making a Difference
189

ACKNOWLEDGMENTS

A book of this kind dealing with all types of social and economic features for many companies and industries would not be possible without the research input of others. Some of those who have made particularly valuable contributions include, but are by no means restricted to, John Fairbanks, Jr., Steve Heim, Peter Lowry, Susan Meeker-Lowry, and Carol Trenga-Schein. More than a decade ago, in the early days of the socially responsible investing movement, there were those who inspired me and introduced me to the idea of alternative economics. Robert Schwartz, Tim Smith, and Bob Swann were especially encouraging and helpful. At Boston College, Severyn Bruyn has been researching the concept of a social economy for more than two decades.

My thanks to Shirley Urban, who did an exceptional job of making what seemed at times like massive changes in the several drafts of this book. My special thanks to my editor Dan Conaway, who showed me how to write understandable English, not sociologese. He and Ed Barber at W. W. Norton also had the vision to see that this book could make a difference by persuading others that social investing is more than just a good thing to do: It can also be very profitable economically.

PROLOGUE

About eighteen years ago my parents died, and I found myself executor for an estate, most in the form of traditional stock and bond investments accumulated by my father, who had been a senior partner for a California-based brokerage firm. I also found that I would be responsible for the management of these investments.

As a youngster I grew up in a family that talked about money and investments, and in the later years of their lives as cotrustee I helped my parents manage their investments. Therefore, the world of money was not a complete mystery. Nevertheless, I had spent most of my life as a social scientist far from the business world. To compensate, I took a self-directed crash course in the stock and bond markets.

I had heard about the rapidly growing movement of socially and ethically concerned investors who used their shareholder power to influence corporate practices, and I decided to take a portion of the family's inheritance and apply various ethical and social standards, in addition to traditional economic criteria, to investment decisions. For several years I tracked the performance of the family's socially screened investments against the performance of the traditional investments. To my surprise, and to the surprise of some professional money managers with whom I worked, the social investments, as a whole, outperformed the traditional investments in total return.

I decided to turn my full-time scholarly focus on the history, philosophy, and consequences of ethical and social investing. This book is testimony to two rather astonishing—and seemingly paradoxical—facts: that socially responsible investing (SRI) and socially responsible business practices can pay off very handsomely relative to investments and business conduct done solely "for profit" and that social investments and socially responsible companies can weather difficult economic times better than their "profit only" counterparts.

A friend once described purely academic writing as dropping a feather down a well and listening for the splash. After years of work, a scholar is lucky if a few thousand copies of a book on an obscure topic are sold or if several colleagues comment upon a specialized article for a professional journal. That had certainly been my experience with many of the articles and books I had written. In contrast, the response to my first semipopular article, entitled "Social Investing: Doing Good while Doing Well," for the *Futurist* magazine, was overwhelming. I received telephone calls and letters from all over the world, from Tokyo to Rio de Janeiro. All asked for more information about socially good companies that were also good economic investments. Clearly I had touched a sensitive nerve and uncovered a big need.

In 1982 I founded a small publishing company in Vermont with my son. Since that time GOOD MONEY Publications, Inc., has published newsletters, handbooks, and other materials for all kinds of ethically and socially concerned investors. Our company has also screened portfolios for individual and institutional investors for a variety of positive and negative social factors, including good employee and environmental records, programs for minorities and women, nuclear weapons production, and support for repressive regimes, such as the South African government. This book contains many examples and illustrations of the kinds of investment opportunities our company's research has discovered.

Any book about investing runs risks. Things can change very quickly in the marketplace. Several years ago a solar energy entrepreneur started a book on investing in the stocks of solar energy companies. Then along came "tax reform." Tax credits for homeowners installing solar energy systems were eliminated, and government funding for projects dried up. An unexpected product disaster or an executive caught skimming money can quickly turn yesterday's corporate hero into tomorrow's goat. Therefore, the socially responsible companies cited in this book are not being nominated for lifetime sainthood. Nor are they being applauded for present-day perfection. There is no such thing as a permanent good bet in investing. If there were, everyone would be a millionaire. All the companies and investments cited in this book—and many more could have been cited—are merely used as examples of past opportunities for socially concerned investors.

In addition, as any financial adviser would observe, past financial performance is no guarantee of future financial performance. Therefore, neither the positive or negative examples of investment nor corporate performance used in this book are recommendations for any particular future investment action. Rather, they are used as examples of the ways in which socially responsible investing pays off better than traditional profit-only investing.

Perhaps the most exciting and promising aspect of socially responsible investing is that it represents a positive alternative to the usual ways of doing business and making money. This alternative is summarized perfectly in an ancient Eastern (note, *not* Western) story of a man who was given permission to see both heaven and hell while he was still alive. He first chose to see hell. He found, to his surprise, an enormous gathering of people at a feast. Each was seated at a long table, covered with every imaginable delicacy. Nevertheless, the people were crying and wailing loudly, and they all appeared to be starving to death. As the man looked over this scene, he saw that the handles of the eating utensils were so long that the people at the table could not bring the food to their mouths. With a heavy heart, the man left hell to visit heaven, where he found an almost identical scene: a table laden with food and utensils with long handles. But these people were laughing and rejoicing. Rather than trying to feed only themselves, the people in heaven were feeding each other.

GOOD MONEY

I

MAKING MONEY
THE NEW-FASHIONED
WAY

For as many years as Wall Street has housed the New York Stock Exchange, Wall Street has offered one consistent piece of investment advice: Don't mix money and morality. The first order of business, even for socially concerned individuals, is to maximize return on investment. Once the investor or corporation has secured a nest egg or adequate profits, *then* social concerns can be addressed—particularly in the form of tax-deductible donations to favorite charities and social action organizations.

Often, though, this logic allows—indeed, *encourages*—the investor and business executive to cast a blind eye toward the means of securing that nest egg or profit. No one need worry about whether or not Multicorp A has an unacceptable environmental record or has consistently failed to promote women and minorities into senior executive positions or spends most of its energy on the production of nuclear weapons. If you're concerned about such issues, Wall Street advises you to make charitable contributions, write letters to your senators, and recycle your newspapers and bottles, but, please, keep your investment and business decisions separate from ethical and social decisions.

During the Vietnam War increasing numbers of investors and

businesspeople felt they could no longer follow that advice, and the socially responsible investment movement was born. Since that time it has grown exponentially in numbers of individuals, businesses, and organizations involved—and in the amount of money involved, which has been estimated by some to be between $500 billion and $1 trillion in the United States alone. SRI is also growing rapidly in Europe. The movement includes three related but somewhat different approaches: ethical investing, social investing, and alternative investing.

Though most concerned investors and businesspeople use a combination of these three strategies, they are distinct in that they range from more passive to more active roles, from more economically conventional to more economically nontraditional practices, and from investments involving smaller social and economic risks to those involving greater social and economic risks. However, the various strategies employed by ethical, social, and alternative investors and businesspeople all share several aspects. First, they are part of a strategy that was best summarized by President Franklin D. Roosevelt at the height of the U.S. depression in 1936: "We have always known that heedless self-interest was bad morals; we know now that it is bad economics." Second, the three strategies reflect a philosophy that strikingly distinguishes them from traditional, competitive business practices. This philosophy was expressed by the Indian leader Mohandas K. Gandhi when he was asked about the difference between nonviolence as a political weapon and the use of force: "My noncooperation is noncooperation with evil, not with the evil-doer." In other words, Gandhi's targets were not groups of people or individuals; they were evil systems and institutions. For example, those who ask U.S. corporations to withdraw from South Africa are not trying to hurt corporate executives or employees. They are asking that those corporations not give support to a racist and repressive political system.

Socially concerned investors include not only individuals who support ethically acceptable (and avoid ethically offensive) investments but also business managers who use their economic power to implement needed social programs and practices. The dictionary defines *investing* as putting money to use, by purchase or expenditure, in something offering profitable returns. SRI, then, is putting money to use in something that offers profitable returns *and* that actively supports and promotes a higher quality of life, welfare, and social relations in society.

ETHICAL INVESTING: A MATTER OF PRINCIPLE

In many ways, ethical investing is the simplest form of SRI. It involves individual and institutional investors who decide what their most important ethical values are and make their investment decisions reflect those values. It also includes those businesspeople who run their businesses to reflect particular moral values.

For example, in 1978 the Teachers Insurance & Annuity Association of America/College Retirement Equity Fund (TIAA/CREF), the largest pension fund in the country with assets of more than $80 billion by 1989, began adopting new guidelines to avoid investments in companies conducting a major portion of their business in the liquor and tobacco industries. This decision reflected TIAA/CREF's concern for the welfare of college students. In 1986 the fund began divesting companies with operations in South Africa. In response to pressures from some participants to broaden its social screen, TIAA/CREF announced in 1990 that it would offer a CREF Social Choice Account. This accumulated retirement savings account would initially screen by not investing in companies that:

Have economic ties to South Africa

Have operations in Northern Ireland and have not conducted business in compliance with the North Ireland Fair Employment Act of 1989

Produce nuclear energy

Have a significant portion of business involved in the manufacture
of weapons

Manufacture and market alcoholic beverages or tobacco products

In 1982 the Presbyterian Church adopted guidelines for divesting
war-related investments. Divestment targets included:

The ten leading military contractors each year

Major corporations dependent on military contracts for 25 percent
or more of their sales

Makers of key nuclear components for warheads

In 1988 the church announced that investments in twenty-two
companies had been banned from funds held by the Board of
Pensions and the Presbyterian Foundation. These investments,
worth almost $2.5 billion, included such companies as Boeing,
General Dynamics, General Electric, Lockheed, McDonnell
Douglas, Raytheon, and Rockwell International. In addition,
Presbyterian institutions of higher education and regional pres-
byteries and synods were urged to follow the national divestment
policy.

In mid-1988 the General Conference of the United Methodist
Church, the second-largest Protestant denomination in the United
States, strongly endorsed a statement on economic injustice. More
than two-thirds of the nearly 1,000 delegates voted for it. The
statement called for Western countries and banks to bear the bur-
den of resolving the international debt crisis, since large corporations had moved their operations to developing countries to take
advantage of cheaper labor and less stringent laws. The assembly
also called for the divestment of stock in any company doing
business in South Africa.

In 1977 Smith College's Investment Committee prepared
questionnaires which it mailed to the companies whose stock the
college owned. The questionnaires asked about the companies'
policies in South Africa. When no satisfactory answer was received
from Firestone Tire and Rubber, Smith College sold more than

42,000 shares of stock worth about $688,000 at the time. Ironically, this action resulted in Smith College's avoiding a future loss. Shortly after the sale Firestone received bad publicity for its cover-up and for its denial of serious defects in its 500-radial brand tire. Though the stock had been dropping for several years, it continued its plunge until it reached a low of slightly more than $6 per share in 1980. Thus, Smith College avoided a future potential loss of more than 60 percent in the value of the holding.

Ethical investors, however, do not simply bypass offensive investments. New Hampshire-based Pax World Fund not only avoids defense contractors, nuclear utilities, and alcohol, tobacco, and gambling companies but also seeks out companies producing "life-supportive" products and services. In addition, Pax World—started by Quakers and Methodists—looks for companies with good records in equal opportunity employment and pollution control. By mid-1990 Pax World had more than $105 million of total net assets under management in stocks, bonds, and other investment instruments. Stock investments have included companies such as Abbott Labs, Consolidated Natural Gas, Merck & Company, Pacific Lighting, and Walt Disney. The fund also looks for investments in certificates of deposit for local banks—banks that keep their deposits within local communities for development needs, such as Indian Head Bank of Portsmouth, New Hampshire. For most concerned investors, U.S. Treasury instruments are anathema, since the revenue received from their sale goes into the general treasury and may be used to fund such activities as CIA involvement around the world as well as the national war-making potential. As a consequence, the government investments favored by Pax World Fund have included instruments of the Federal Home Loan Bank, Federal National Mortgage Association, and International Bank for Reconstruction & Development.

Every year, in order to create more public awareness of corporations that have developed a sense of social responsibility, the New York City–based Council on Economic Priorities (CEP) nominates U.S. companies for outstanding performance in a number of areas of social concern. A panel of judges then votes a winner in each category. For 1989 nineteen companies were nominated in five categories. The awards were presented to the winners on March 2. The following were the nominees and winners (in italics) in each of the 1989 categories:

CATEGORY	WINNER AND RUNNERS-UP	WINNER'S POLICY/PROGRAM
Charitable contributions	*Dayton Hudson,* Apple Computer, H. B. Fuller, Newman's Own, Tom's of Maine	Pioneered a 5 percent giving policy in 1946. Employees at local chains participate in decisions about gifts, which have included a 24-hour domestic abuse hot line and cosponsorship of a conference on AIDS in the workplace.
Community action	*Digital Equipment,* Clorox, Ford Motor, Stride Rite	Has job-training programs, purchases from minorities and women, and has high-tech educational programs for minorities and women.
Employee policies	*Federal Express,* Herman Miller, Pitney Bowes, Stride Rite	Has a no-layoff policy and offers a variety of incentives. Has an appeals process for problems that cannot be resolved between employees and supervisors.
Environment	*Applied Energy Services,* AT&T, Clorox, The Body Shop, H. B. Fuller	Created innovative way to balance the potentially harmful effects of coal burning in one of its power plants by donating $2 million toward the planting of 52 million trees in Guatemala to combat the greenhouse effect.
Equal opportunity	*Eastman Kodak,* Bristol Myers,* Digital Equipment, Harbor Sweets, Nordstrom	One-fourth of purchasing goes to small businesses owned by women, minorities, and the handicapped.

*Before the company became Bristol-Myers Squibb.

Honorable mention also was given to two companies for exceptional programs and policies. H. B. Fuller was honored for its consistently good environmental record over the years. In 1971 the company donated 95 acres of land as a wildlife preserve when it built new headquarters outside Minneapolis. Many years ago

END OF 1980 TO END OF 1988
Change in

COMPANY	TOTAL SALES/ REVENUES	NET PROFIT	PRINCIPAL PRODUCTS/SERVICES
Apple Computer	+3,377%	+3,321%	Computers
Federal Express	+835	+385	Overnight package delivery
Nordstrom	+471	+526	Fashion specialty stores
Digital Equipment	+385	+423	Computers
Herman Miller	+210	+269	Office furniture
Dayton Hudson	+201	+99	Department stores
H. B. Fuller	+131	+118	Adhesives, sealants, and paints
Stride Rite	+128	+451	Children's, sporting, and work shoes and boots
Ford Motor	+122	+443	Automobiles
Pitney Bowes	+111	+216	Postage and mailing meters and equipment
Clorox	+98	+299	Bleach products
Bristol Myers†	+89	+206	Pharmaceuticals
Eastman Kodak	+75	+21	Cameras
Average	+142%	+147%*	

*Not including Ford Motor, which had a large loss in 1980 and a substantial profit in 1988. If net profit for Ford were incorporated, this number would be even larger. All the other companies nominated by CEP in 1989 had positive net profits in 1980.

†Before the company became Bristol-Myers Squibb.

the company (makers of paints, adhesives, and sealants) switched from solvent-based chemicals (which are harmful to the environment) to water-based adhesives, and in 1986 the company adopted a worldwide environmental safety policy.

Newman's Own, founded by actor Paul Newman, was honored because all the profits of the company are donated to charitable causes, such as the Hole-in-the-Wall Gang Camp for children with life-threatening diseases, a camp Newman helped found. In addition, the company's food products (salad dressing, popcorn, and spaghetti sauce) are made from natural ingredients and packaged primarily in biodegradable materials.

As the above table shows, the positive social programs and policies of these companies has had no visible negative impact upon their bottom lines. Thirteen of the publicly traded companies nominated by CEP in 1989 had more than $144 billion in total sales or revenues in 1988, an increase of 142 percent since the end of 1980. Twelve of the nominated companies had a 1988

net profit of almost $5 billion, an increase of 147 percent for the
same period of time.

SOCIAL INVESTING: A MATTER OF CHANGE

In contrast with ethical investing—which is a relatively "passive"
approach to social responsibility—social investing involves direct
economic and political action to change economic practices. When
the Securities and Exchange Commission (SEC) was created in
1934, one of its mandates was to assure that shareholders could
exercise their voting rights. In 1942 the SEC ruled that management had to publish in its proxy statement any items it knew
would come up for consideration at the annual meeting. Yet fil-
ing shareholder resolutions—a very direct way of letting corporations know what individual and institutional investors think of
company policy—is a relatively recent tactic.

In the 1970s socially concerned investors adopted the shareholder proxy process. The first "social resolutions" dealt with issues
such as requesting Dow Chemical to stop the production of napalm
and General Motors to include more minorities on the company's board of directors. Some companies contested the right of
shareholders to raise what they felt were purely "social" (not business) issues, but the courts and the SEC ruled that social issues
were a legitimate concern of all shareholders. The number of
shareholder "social resolutions" filed jumped from 30 in 1972 to
between 100 and 200 in each year from 1976 to 1988. Church
groups became particularly active in raising questions about war
production, nuclear power, and human rights. Conservative
organizations sponsored proxies asking corporations not to deal
with Communist countries. Some large institutional investors
(including banks, insurance companies, universities, and pension funds) started developing elaborate procedures for evaluating
shareholder proposals. They no longer blindly followed the Wall
Street "wisdom" that management always knows best how to run
the business.

In January 1988 the Interfaith Center for Corporate Responsibility (ICCR) reported that it had assisted its members to sponsor more than 150 shareholder resolutions with more than 120 companies. These individual and institutional investors were worth more than $250 billion. By 1990 some of those figures had increased dramatically. In that year ICCR reported that more than 300 resolutions had been filed with more than 180 companies by more than 260 socially concerned investors and organizations worth more than $500 billion. The sponsors included religious groups, state and city pension funds, TIAA/CREF, a Canadian religious shareholder action organization, a school district, social action groups, a union, and organizations involved in the SRI movement. The table on page 28 lists the primary areas of social concern and the number of 1990 proxies reported on by ICCR. Figures in parentheses reflect those resolutions that were disallowed by the Securities and Exchange Commission, rejected for technical reasons (incorrectly written), or withdrawn because the sponsors had reached agreements with management about the issue concerned.

Until 1988 concerned investors sponsoring shareholder proxies operated under the assumption that their proxies would never pass if they were opposed by management; generally that assumption was correct. Nevertheless, shareholders were content with 3 to 5 percent of the total votes and the frequent media attention their proxies received. In fact, most corporate managers take shareholder proxies seriously. They are concerned that their annual meetings run smoothly, that controversy be avoided, and that most, if not all, shareholders are supportive of company policies and practices. Often, as a result of the increase in votes received by shareholder resolutions, management will meet with concerned shareholders before the annual meeting in an attempt to reach some sort of compromise. This is what happened when church groups asked First National Bank of Boston not to make loans to South Africa. The first resolution received less than 5 percent of all votes. The next year bank officials met with the church shareholders and agreed not to renew any existing loans or grant any new loans, and a similar resolution was withdrawn by the church groups. The same type of agreement was reached

1990 SHAREHOLDER RESOLUTIONS
(as of January 29, 1990)

Many companies had more than one shareholder proxy, all of which dealt with different social issues. For example, American Express had three proxies asking for an employment practices report, adoption of environmental principles, and cessation of sales of products, services, and technologies in South Africa. Because of the Alaskan oil spill, Exxon led with eleven proxies, which asked for everything from the replacement of the chief executive officer to the use of state-of-the-art ship design. Other proxies dealt with special problems that companies were having. Burlington Northern was challenged for using its railroad rights-of-way for the transportation of MX missiles. U.S. Surgical was asked to stop spying on animal rights activists who advocated alternatives to the use of animals for product testing.

South Africa—125 (17)
No sales or services	110(16)
Report on policies there	10 (1)
Adopt equaiity principles	5

Environment—63 (16)
Adopt policies	31 (4)
Report problems	18 (6)
Clean up hazards	12 (5)
Eliminate Styrofoam	1 (1)
Pay victims of gas leak	1

North Ireland—29
Adopt equality principles	20
Report policies there	9

Employee Policies—18 (11)
Housing for employees	9 (7)
Report policies	8 (3)
Health and safety standards	1 (1)

Military and Defense—16 (4)
Weapons work*	10 (4)
Economic conversion	4
Government contracts	2

Debt Crisis—13 (3)
Reduce international debt	9
Report international debt	2(1)
Involvement with farm debt	2 (2)

Corporate Governance—11 (1)
Campaign finance reform	7
Provide for secret ballot	3(1)
Replace CEO	1

Animal Rights—9
Reduce animal testing	7
Report animal testing	1
Stop spying on critics	1

Third World—7 (2)
Infant formula sales	3(1)
Equality in foreign operations	2(1)
Status of women employees	2

Tobacco—6
No sales after 1999	3
Report sales to minors	1
Report lobbying	1
Stop making cigarette papers	1

Affirmative Action—4 (1)
Integrate board of directors	3(1)
Minority business contracts	1

*Nuclear, chemical, biological, and "Star Wars."

when Central Maine Power agreed to pursue conservation measures over power plant construction.

By 1988 some shareholder proxies had begun receiving a significant portion of the votes cast at annual corporate meetings. A proposal for confidential voting procedures received one-third of all the votes at Phelps Dodge, more than 20 percent at Honey-well, and more than 19 percent at Lockheed. At CBI Industries a proposal to sign a statement of fair employment principles for the company's South African operations received 23 percent of all votes cast. The influence of shareholder proposals on manage-ment is indicated in the following figures for how many compa-nies in the United States withdrew from doing business in South Africa from 1984 through 1989:

YEAR ENDING	NUMBER OF U.S. COMPANIES IN SOUTH AFRICA OR NAMBIA*	Change	
		YEARLY	CUMULATIVE
1984	317	—	—
1985	277	−13%	−13%
1986	225	−19	−29
1987	169	−25	−47
1988	142	−16	−55
1989	124	−13	−61

*Having direct investments.

Some startling successes are possible even with the most hard-nosed of corporate managers. In the 1970s the Sisters of Loretto, the oldest Catholic women's order in North America, targeted the Blue Diamond Coal Mining Company for action. Blue Dia-mond had become known to socially concerned investors as the "J. P. Stevens of Appalachia." One of the largest coal producers in eastern Kentucky, the company had a history of safety viola-tions and neglect of public demands for accountability. Through the 1970s Blue Diamond had been continually cited by govern-ment agencies for safety violations; it was responsible for a meth-ane gas explosion that killed twenty-six miners, and it caused pollution that required two cities to close their water systems.

Under the 1934 SEC Act, a company with fewer than 500 shareholders was not required to file public information about its operations. Blue Diamond had taken the necessary actions to protect this "privilege," including buying out small shareholders when it appeared that public ownership was approaching the 500 mark. In the early 1980s, with the help of Shearson / American Express broker Robert J. Schwartz, members of the order's investment committee initiated a stock-purchasing plan to push Blue Diamond's public ownership beyond 500. The order became one of the principals and the first stock purchasers in the Blue Diamond Coal Company Monitoring Project. The project asked 300 concerned individuals to buy just one share of stock each. At the time the company's stock was selling for around $200 per share on the over-the-counter market.

Blue Diamond's management responded by refusing to register the stock for the new owners, arguing that the purchases had been made for reasons that had nothing to do with economic profit. The project sued Blue Diamond, demanding that the new owners be registered. The company responded with a deposition requiring the disclosure of the names, addresses, and affiliations of social activists throughout the South—an obvious attempt at political intimidation.

The project legally challenged Blue Diamond's deposition and was successful in getting the court to quash it. The company then dropped its refusal to register new shareholders, but the project sued Blue Diamond for legal fees and damages for the considerable costs incurred. The court ruled in favor of the project, supporting the right of shareholders to purchase stock for both economic and social reasons:

> The record clearly shows that the plaintiffs [Loretto Literary & Benevolent Institution, et al.] simply intended to legally exercise routine shareholder rights in order to lobby their views to management with the expectation of enhancing, not injuring, Blue Diamond. Shareholders have the inherent right to assert their individual interests within their Company, however bizarre, unpopular, or unusual they may be [Court of Chancery of the state of Delaware in and for the New Castle County, March 12, 1982].

The court also directed Blue Diamond to pay all legal fees (damages were not awarded). At the 1982 shareholders meeting it was established that there were 565 shareholders in the company. Therefore, the company was now required to file public information about its operations, and management adopted a more conciliatory and cooperative stance.

Where ethical investing seeks to introduce a moral dimension into investing and business practices, social investing goes one step farther, focusing upon economic and political action to change investing and business practices. Alternative investing, the third SRI strategy, concentrates upon support for atypical and unusual forms of investment and business practices. Two forms of alternative investing typify this strategy of SRI: land trusts and community-based revolving loan funds.

ALTERNATIVE INVESTING: BUSINESS NOT AS USUAL

Until 1987 David Britt was a real estate developer. His father had developed Country Farm Estates in Sandwich, on Cape Cod, Massachusetts. When the 387 acres of land were first purchased in 1972, plans included the development of more than 620 houses or a 440-unit condominium with a championship golf course. The town resisted since the land had long produced some of the best vegetables on Cape Cod when it had been Veg-Acre Farm. Because of a lawsuit, by 1977 only 3 houses had been built on the land, and interest rates continued to climb. Then a compromise was reached. Britt's father sold 228 acres to the Massachusetts Agriculture Preservation Restriction (APR) program. The land was put into restricted farm use, and buildings, strawberry patches, peach and apple trees, and Christmas trees replaced condos, swimming pools, and parking areas.

APR, started in 1977, is the most successful of all the New England farm preservation programs, according to *Yankee* magazine. By 1988 APR had bought the rights to almost 20,000 acres on 219 farms. The state buys the farmer's land for the difference between its value as real estate and its value as a farm, admittedly a lower price than a developer would pay. The farmer keeps the land, though the rights to develop it have been sold. The quality and history of a community's life have been preserved, and urban development lives in some harmony with the natural environment. An interesting footnote to this story is that in 1987 twenty-seven-year-old David Britt quit his job as a real estate developer and began a new career as operator of the preserved Windstar Farm, the largest farm remaining on Cape Cod.

National organizations, such as the Nature Conservancy and the American Farmland Trust, will also work with local land trusts to preserve land. A major goal is to preserve America's rapidly vanishing breadbasket. A 1981 study by the U.S. Department of Agriculture and the Council on Environmental Quality concluded that New Mexico could lose 44 percent of its prime farmland by the year 2000. By then California could lose 21 percent, Washington 23 percent, Pennsylvania 21 percent, West Virginia 23 percent, and Vermont 43 percent. Rhode Island and Florida could be without any of their farmland whatsoever. Indeed, the study estimated that by the start of the twenty-first century, fifteen farm-producing U.S. states could lose a combined 50 percent of prime farmland to condos, shopping centers, and parking lots.

The concept of land trusts has deep roots in American history, going back to the colonial concept of a commons—land held by the community for the common good and use. However, the country was slow to develop and implement the idea because of the value placed on individual ownership of land in a capitalist economy. Two of the oldest land trust organizations were formed in New England about a hundred years ago: Trustees of Reservations and the Society for the Protection of New Hampshire Forests. A 1985 survey found 535 land trusts nationwide with more than 225 in the New England region.

The growth in the popularity of the concept in recent years has been impressive. In 1978 Maine had only a handful of trusts, but by 1985 there were 27, and by 1988 there were 45. There are almost two dozen active land trusts in Vermont. Vermont Land Trust, created in 1977, is the largest. It helps protect more than 25,000 acres of farm, forest, and open-space land worth an estimated $25 million, and its 125 projects range in size from less than an acre on a Lake Champlain island to the 1,600-acre Martin Farms in the White River valley. Part of this growth may be credited to Robert Swann and Ralph Borsodi, who in the 1960s developed the philosophy and legal strategies necessary for land trusts. Today community-based land trusts can lease land through long-term or lifetime contracts to individuals, families, businesses, cooperatives, or community organizations. Lease fees are paid on the basis of use value rather than full-market value. Though the land is not individually owned, buildings and other structures may be, and they can later be sold on the basis of use value (plus inflation and improvements) versus prevailing market value. This represents a significant modification of the traditional concept of a market economy.

Land trusts can be used to rehabilitate and rebuild urban areas as well as preserve rural regions. One such urban land trust is the South Atlanta Land Trust (SALT). More than twenty years ago South Atlanta was a prosperous middle-class African-American community of more than 700 single-family homes, most privately owned. Then, in the 1960s, the area began to decline. Clark College and Gammon Seminary relocated. Families moved out, and absentee landlords and businesses started purchasing property. Over a period of three decades more than 200 units of housing were lost, and home ownership dropped to 35 percent in South Atlanta. The South Atlanta Civic League was formed and took emergency action, defeating efforts to condemn its properties and tearing down abandoned houses that were seen as hazards. These measures created a need to put those newly vacant lots to use in order to rebuild South Atlanta.

In 1981 the Civic League began working with the Massachusetts-based Institute for Community Economics (ICE) to form SALT. By early 1988 SALT was involved in five major projects:

Neighborhood Preservation Project: Acquired and renovated vacant houses for moderate-income families, using its own construction crews hired through minority subcontractors. Two local banks provided innovative lending.

Low-income Housing Project: Moved and rehabilitated eight houses scheduled for demolition as a result of a noise abatement program at

Atlanta's airport. An ICE loan funded the moving of the houses to a large lot in South Atlanta.

Cooperative Housing Project: Acquired Gammon Seminary's former student housing and was rehabilitating it for the elderly and young mothers with small children. After rehabilitation was completed, the project was to be organized into a limited equity cooperative.

New Construction Project: Constructed three-bedroom homes for moderate- and low-income families, the first new construction in South Atlanta in twenty years.

Operation New Start: Had houses moved from the airport free of charge by some of Atlanta's home movers to provide transitional housing for homeless families in South Atlanta.

Atlanta's Mayor Andrew Young was quoted as saying that SALT is a "united community effort" drawing upon "all of the resources that are available: that's human resources, city resources, religious community resources and neighborhood resources." In this cooperative sense, it is an example of alternative investing at its best. SALT not only successfully provided low-cost housing to low- and moderate-income people but also rehabilitated a decaying neighborhood and provided one answer to the problem of homelessness.

One device for financing the cooperatives, land trusts, and other programs of alternative investors is the community-based revolving loan fund. One book on the subject describes in detail twenty-five such funds in seventeen states, ranging from California to Vermont and including the District of Columbia. Though each fund has different goals and purposes, they share the common goal of preserving and rehabilitating land and housing, particularly for moderate- and low-income citizens. The projects are designed to provide jobs and foster a sense of cooperation and self-help on the part of those who are in need of help.

Opportunities for socially concerned investors also vary from fund to fund. However, the practice of the Low-Income Housing Fund in California is fairly typical. An investment is placed in a certificate of deposit (CD) that earns the prevailing market rate of interest. However, the returns from the CD are split between the investor and the nonprofit housing development corporation. In other words, socially concerned investors are willing to take a return that is slightly under the going market rate in order to permit the fund to subsidize the interest rate of the underlying loan and make available housing to those who might not otherwise be able to afford it. Why would investors be willing to take slightly less than the market rate of interest? Since its founding in 1984 through January 1987, the Low-Income Housing Fund made twelve loans totaling $822,000, which created 419 housing units, and this fund never had a default. Indeed, the default record of the country's revolving loan funds, which make housing available to poor people, would be the envy of many major American banks. This record is something many investors in America's savings and loans would have appreciated.

Some large corporations are beginning to demonstrate a willingness to take greater investment risks for things that are deemed socially valuable. The New York Life Insurance Company announced in May 1988 that it would invest more than $8 million to fund the work of the IDEC Pharmaceuticals Corporation on AIDS-related anti-idiotype technology—the use of human-made antibodies to diagnose and treat diseases. IDEC's first product, for treating lymphatic cancer, was being clinically tested. New York Life received warrants to purchase IDEC preferred stock and will receive royalties on the sales of all AIDS-related products that may be developed. This was the first AIDS treatment venture capital investment by a life insurance company. Commenting for New York Life, a spokesperson told the *Wall Street Journal* that the investment was partially to fulfill the company's corporate responsibility and partially a follow-up to an overall investment strategy. It was a decision that was both socially sound and economically prudent.

Large institutional investors are also beginning to show interest in local community development. In mid-1988 the *Wall Street Journal* reported that some of the country's biggest pension and retirement funds had initiated programs to finance rehabilitation efforts. From 1981 to 1988 New York City's pension funds invested $300 million for moderate- and low-income housing. The Massachusetts state pension board agreed to put $50 million into affordable housing, including apartments in an abandoned warehouse in Boston's working-class Charlestown district. Connecticut's state pension plan lent $475 million for in-state mortgages. Pension and retirement funds represent a potential $3 trillion resource for such investments. Skeptics of such social investing by these funds argue that it limits the ability of a fund to obtain the highest rate of return for fund members, who rely upon the fund for their retirement. In response, New York City's comptroller told the *Wall Street Journal* that the pension fund's housing investments had yielded from 11 to 13 percent annually, the same return that could have been obtained from traditional fixed-income investments made for profit potential only. The key is, again, cooperation. To generate this rate of return, pension funds must have available subsidies, federal guarantees, and tax breaks. As was the case with SALT, cooperation between all public and private levels is essential.

2

THE FINANCIAL
EXPERTS VS. SRI

As the examples of shareholder action indicate, SRI certainly works socially. SRI can move corporations to change policies and practices, and perhaps more important, it can foster public awareness about the need to use economic resources creatively to resolve major social problems.

Does SRI work economically? Can businesses make a profit and investors receive a satisfactory return while taking into account social factors when making business and investment decisions? There is increasing evidence that the answer to these questions is often a resounding yes. The evidence can be seen in the generally poor financial record for most traditional money managers compared with the sometimes spectacular record for some socially screened investments.

THOSE UNDERPERFORMING
INVESTMENT EXPERTS

The record of performance for financial experts, as a whole, has not been good. In 1979 the *Wall Street Journal* reported on a study of a representative sample of 571 pension and profit-sharing funds containing both equity and bond investments, for varying periods ranging up to fifteen years. The average performance for these funds fell far short of matching both the average inflation rate and the average rate of return on cash equivalents, such as treasury bills. This poor average held true whether the period was three, five, ten, or fifteen years. As Burton Malkiel, author of *A Random Walk down Wall Street*, has summarized it, "Over long periods of time two-thirds of professional investments are outperformed by an unmanaged broad-based stock index. Eighty percent of the investment pros were outperformed by the S&P's 500 during the first half of 1987."

Such a poor performance by financial managers can have an impact far beyond mere return to investors. In 1980 a bipartisan Northeast-Northwest Congressional Coalition announced that the manner in which pension funds were invested actually accelerated unemployment and plant closings in economically troubled areas of the country. Fund managers, seeking the highest possible short-term rate of return, favored boomtown regions in the American Sunbelt and Southwest and avoided investments in firms and corporations in the North and Middle West. Therefore, the earnings and savings of workers contributing to pension and retirement funds in these latter regions were being used in a way that could threaten their future employment if corporations decided to close down plants and move to the boomtown regions. Ironically, some of the Sunbelt regions were to turn from boom to bust only a few short years later.

Part of the problem for financial experts is information overload. One brokerage house executive expressed his frustration in attempts to advise his clients about oil and gas stocks: "I don't know what to tell them. Heck, I can't tell whether a discovery in the Overthrust Belt is more important than one in Louisiana. We try to go after [fundamental information], but still it's like flipping a coin." At the same time, nowhere more than in the financial and economic worlds are fictitious and biased numbers used. Consider, for example, the well-known Dow Jones stock averages. These are nothing more than imaginary abstractions of the

New York Stock Exchange as a whole, and many analysts believe that as such they are not very good abstractions. Only thirty companies at any one time appear on the Dow Jones Industrial Average (DJIA), and at any given time, whole industries may be missing from representation. On the 1988 DJIA, no companies appeared for the industrial services, publishing, real estate, or recreation industries, all significant segments of the modern economy. Other averages, such as the Standard & Poor's 500, are a bit more representative, but they still suffer from the same biases. Yet so real has the DJIA become as a measure of not only what the stock markets are doing but what the economy as a whole is doing that every major news medium shouts its performance daily. Furthermore, over the last decade or so, gambling in stock index futures has become extremely popular, something that many analysts believe led to the extreme market instability during 1987. A gambler can bet on whether or not the S&P 500 is going to go up or down, by a specified amount, during a particular period of time. Such a transaction serves no real market or economic purpose since the bet involves a fictitious basket of stocks that no one really owns and that never changes hands.

In addition, investment experts often utilize popular theories that contain questionable biases. One such is the efficient market theory, which argues that the market always operates in the most efficient manner possible for several reasons. The price of a company's stock merely reflects the value of its future earnings, and all any investor can do is to try to predict these earnings better than other investors. This is difficult (if not impossible), however, since most investors have access to fairly equivalent information sources.

The implication of the efficient market theory is that investors should not try to beat the market. Rather, they should be content merely to stay up with it. Money spent on allegedly better information is money wasted. In 1967 three executives at *Forbes* magazine decided to test this theory by designing what became known as the Dart-Board Fund. They threw darts at the stock-quote pages of the *New York Times* and came up with a list of twenty-eight stocks in which they imaginarily invested $1,000 each. From 1967 to 1979 the Dart-Board Fund grew from $28,000 to $43,279, a gain of almost 55 percent. For the same period of time the Standard & Poor's 500 Index gained a miserly 8.2 percent, while the DJIA actually lost 4 percent in value.

How were the professional money managers doing during this period? Another *Forbes* study analyzed the performance of 109 mutual funds from November 19, 1968, to June 30, 1980. The funds were graded on their performance against one another on a scale of A, B, C, D, or F. *Forbes* reported that for periods when the market was advancing, the funds averaged a barely passing grade of C. For periods of market declines, the funds flunked with an F. The conclusion appears to be that it is costly and useless to attempt to beat the market with expert money management, and coin flipping or dart throwing can sometimes do just as well or better. However, there are several things wrong with the efficient market theory and the *Forbes* test of that theory.

First, as anyone who understands the laws of chance knows, if one throws twenty-eight darts, he or she has an equal chance of coming up with twenty-eight bad choices as twenty-eight good choices. *Forbes*'s executives lucked out on their first throw. Second, and more important, the efficient market theory is basically flawed. It assumes a rational process in the marketplace, where most investors make the same kinds of thoughtful decisions using the same kinds of information. Reality teaches something quite different. Many, if not most, investors and financial experts make poor decisions, using partial or biased information and flawed theories. In addition, the pressure to perform has led to what has been called the herd instinct in investing.

The prevalence of this herd instinct in the marketplace is a function of some major changes that have taken place in the financial community in recent years—particularly the rise of professionalism. The pressure on professional fund managers to measure continually their performance against the performances of other professional money managers is so great that they tend to follow the crowd. By doing what every other fund manager is doing, they can't be charged with taking unusual risks with a client's money. More important, it can be argued that if the market does go down—and the fund's performance drops—it's the market's fault, not the fund manager's fault. If the market goes up, everyone is happy, and minor differences in improved performance can be easily overlooked.

The herd instinct has a long historical precedent. The concept called the prudent man principle goes back to a Massachusetts Supreme Court ruling in the nineteenth century that argued that a manager of money could not be sued for having been imprudent if that manager was simply doing what all other people of prudence were doing. Since that time many trustees and money managers have continually used this principle as an excuse for their investment behavior. If they simply mimic the behavior of their peers and do what everyone else is doing, they cannot be charged with financial mismanagement. Indeed, the prudent principle has been cited by many money managers as the reason why they cannot become involved in social investing: Other people "of prudence" aren't doing it. However, as some critics have pointed out, there is more to slavish worship of the prudence principle than merely playing it safe. This principle can be used to continue to channel billions of investment dollars into the *Fortune* 500 companies, whether or not these companies are managed well, produce safe and life-supportive goods and services, and have good records for employee relations, the local community, and the environment. In this way, the corporate rich get richer and the competitors and investment alternatives get ignored.

DESIGNING A "GOOD DOW"

Organized SRI has been around for at least several decades. During that time the investment markets have gone through both some of the greatest roaring bull markets and biggest bear markets in history. This provides an opportunity to see how SRI does in both good and bad times.

The longest-running, continuous measure of SRI performance are two stock averages used by GOOD MONEY Publications. One is an average consisting of the stocks of thirty socially acceptable industrial companies. The other is an average consisting of the stocks of fifteen socially acceptable utility companies. Both were originally designed around 1979 in order to track their performance over time in contrast with the Dow Jones equivalents. This tracking has been continuously done since the end of 1976.

To design what some journalists have called the good Dow, the industry areas appearing on the Dow Jones Industrial Average were examined to identify socially acceptable companies in the same industries. For many industries (such as computers, foods, and pharmaceuticals), socially acceptable alternatives to the Dow companies could easily be found since some companies had obviously excellent records for such social issues as environmental protection, community involvement, or employee programs.

For some industries, however, no socially acceptable company could be found. For example, because of nuclear weapons and other war work, all companies in the aerospace and defense industry are unacceptable. In addition, most companies in some industries, such as metals and mining, often have very poor records on specific social issues, such as environmental protection and worker safety. For the GOOD MONEY Industrial Average (GMIA) companies were chosen from industries that provide life-supportive products and services and that have been consistent favorites

GMIA AND DJIA COMPANIES COMPARED
(as of June 1990)

INDUSTRY	GMIA	DJIA
Aerospace / defense	(none)	Boeing
Apparel	Hartmarx Stride Rite	(none)
Automobiles / trucks	Volvo	General Motors Navistar International
Chemicals	H. B. Fuller Minnesota Mining	Du Pont Minnesota Mining Union Carbide

INDUSTRY	GMIA	DJIA
Computers	Digital Equipment Wang Labs	IBM
Electrical equipment / household appliances	Maytag	General Electric Westinghouse
Financial services / banking	First Virginia Banks	American Express
Food / restaurants	Hershey Foods McDonald's	Coca-Cola McDonald's
Forest products	Consolidated Papers	International Paper
Household products	(none)	Procter & Gamble
Industrial services	FlightSafety Int'l.	(none)
Machinery / machine tools	Ametek, Inc. Norton Company Snap-on Tools Zurn Industries	(none)
Metals / mining	(none)	Alcoa
Multiform / conglomerate	(none)	Allied Signal Primerica United Technologies
Office equipment / supplies	A. T. Cross Herman Miller Pitney Bowes	(none)
Petroleum products	(none)	Chevron Exxon Texaco
Pharmaceuticals	Johnson & Johnson	Merck & Company
Precision instruments	Polaroid	Eastman Kodak
Publishing	Meredith Corporation *Washington Post*	(none)
Real estate	Rouse Company	(none)
Recreation	Walt Disney	(none)
Retail stores	Dayton Hudson Melville Corporation	Sears, Roebuck Woolworth
Steel	Worthington Inds.	Bethlehem Steel USX Corp.
Telecommunications	MCI Communications	AT&T
Tires / rubber	(none)	Goodyear
Tobacco	(none)	Philip Morris

of socially concerned investors. The table on pages 42 and 43 compares the GMIA and DJIA companies in mid-1990.

Since 1976 no companies on the GMIA have been replaced for performance reasons. Replacements are made for the same reasons that companies are replaced on the DJIA: The company goes private, the company is merged with another company, or the company goes bankrupt. In other words, a company is replaced when its stock is no longer publicly traded or when it is merged with a company that does not meet socially acceptable standards. Replacements for the GMIA do differ from those for the DJIA in one important way, however: If a company seriously stubs its toes socially, it is replaced with a socially acceptable alternative, even though the offending company may have had a better long-term performance record. Insofar as possible, replacements are made in the same industry category. These are some of the companies which have appeared in the past on the GMIA and the reasons for their being dropped:

COMPANY	REASON DROPPED
Aetna Life & Casualty	Had some serious claims problems
American Greetings	Refused to answer inquiry about community program
Browning-Ferris Industries	Illegal toxic waste dumping and restraint of trade violations
Esquire	Purchased by Gulf + Western, a socially unacceptable conglomerate
General Motors	Serious product quality problems and nuclear weapons work
Levi Strauss	Went private
Norton Simon	Purchased by Esmark, which is not publicly traded
Waste Management	Illegal toxic waste dumping

GOOD MONEY's Utility Average (GMUA) was designed in much the same way to reflect the types of utility companies that appear on the Dow Jones Utility Average (DJUA). Particularly important were companies with no nuclear power connection, or companies developing or using alternative and renewable energy resources (geothermal, wind, solar, biomass), companies with cogeneration and conservation programs, and companies using traditional fossil fuels but having good environmental protection records. The accompanying table compares the GMUA and DJUA companies, as of mid-1990:

GMUA AND DJUA COMPANIES COMPARED
(as of June 1990)

TYPE OF COMPANY	GMUA	DJUA
Diversified services	Citizens Utilities[1]	(none)
Natural gas	Consolidated Nat. Gas Southwest Gas	Columbia Gas System Consolidated Nat. Gas Panhandle Eastern Peoples Energy
Nonnuclear electric utilities[2]	Hawaiian Elec. Inds. Idaho Power Kansas Power & Light Louisville Gas & Elec.* Magma Power Montana Power Oklahoma Gas & Elec. Orange & Rockland Otter Tail Power Southwestern Pub. Svc. TECO Energy	(none)
Nuclear utilities[3]	(none)	American Elec. Power (9%) Centerior Energy (38%) Commonwealth Edison (83%) Consolidated Edison (32%) Detroit Edison (10%) Houston Industries (5%) Niagara Mohawk Power (5%) Pacific Gas & Electric (13%) Philadelphia Electric (35%) Pub. Svc. Enterprises (36%) SCEcorp. (21%)
Water services	United Water Resources	(none)

[1] "B" stock. Company provides electric, gas, telephone, water, and waste water services. Electricity needs are purchased.

[2] With good environmental records and/or developing/using alternative and renewable energy sources, such as biomass, geothermal, hydro, and wind. Also, companies involved in cogeneration and conservation programs.

[3] Percentages in parentheses refer to recent nuclear power generation as portion of total electricity fuel sources.

*Now LG&E Energy Corp.

Replacements have been made since 1976 for the same reasons replacements are made on the GMIA. These are some examples:

COMPANY	REASON DROPPED
American Water Works	Had environmental problems
Pacific Gas & Electric	Refused to abandon Diablo Canyon nuclear plant. Otherwise, an excellent record for energy mix plus use of renewable energy sources
SCEcorp	Had problems with San Onofre nuclear plants. Originally on GMUA for development of solar power
Washington Water Power	Financial involvement with bankrupt nuclear Washington Public Power Supply System. Originally on GMUA because of hydroelectric power generation

The GMIA makes it possible to make direct comparisons between SRI and more traditional investment strategies. It also provides evidence against the Wall Street belief that making social decisions causes an investor to minimize return. The DJIA has included many companies that are simply not acceptable on social grounds, such as Bethlehem Steel (bad pollution record), Boeing (war work), and General Motors (nuclear weapons work). GOOD MONEY's alternatives to these types of companies clearly stand out for various social reasons. How do these companies compare over time in terms of performance?

THE GOOD DOWS OUTPERFORM THE MARKET AND THE EXPERTS

Over the long term (a decade plus) the GMIA consistently and significantly outperformed the DJIA in return to investors. As the accompanying tables show, from the end of 1976 to the end of 1989, the GMIA soared 647 percent in value, compared with a modest increase for the DJIA of 174 percent. Over the years the GMIA has outperformed the DJIA in *both* bull and bear markets. During the bull market of 1987 the DJIA reached an all-time high of 2722.42 (up 171 percent since 1976) on August 25, while the GMIA reached an all-time high of 201.57 (up over 626 percent) on October 1. Then the slide began. By October 16 (the Friday before Bloody Monday) the DJIA had lost 17.5 percent of its value, while the GMIA had lost 15 percent of its value. On Bloody Monday the DJIA shed another 22.6 percent, while the GMIA shed only 15.7 percent of its value. The same better performance occurred during the one-day stock market crash in 1989. On October 13 the GMIA lost 8.46 points, down 3.9 percent, compared with the DJIA, which lost 190.58 points, down 6.9 percent. From 1976 through 1989 the GMIA has outperformed the DJIA by around four to one for the thirteen-year period in both up and down markets.

Comparisons for the GOOD MONEY and Dow utilities show similarly favorable results. From the end of 1976 to the end of 1989 the GMUA climbed 225.6 percent, while the DJUA was up only 116.9 percent. During early 1987 utility stocks fell out of favor as speculators raced to other stock investments. As a result, the GMUA and DJUA began to slide. By the end of 1987, however, the GMUA had lost only 11.5 percent of its value for the

	Good Money Industrial Average			Dow Jones Industrial Average		
		Change			Change	
YEAR	VALUE	FROM LAST YEAR	CUMULATIVE	VALUE	FROM LAST YEAR	CUMULATIVE
1976	27.74	—	—	1004.65	—	—
1977	30.16	+8.7%	+8.7%	831.17	−17.3%	−17.3%
1978	33.62	+11.5	+21.2	805.01	−3.2	−19.9
1979	40.41	+20.2	+45.7	838.74	+4.2	−16.5
1980	49.01	+21.2	+76.7	963.99	+14.9	−4.1
1981	57.83	+18.0	+108.5	875.00	−9.2	−12.9
1982	68.17	+17.9	+145.8	1066.54	+21.9	+6.2
1983	88.20	+29.4	+218.0	1258.64	+18.0	+25.3
1984	84.10	−4.7	+203.2	1211.57	−3.7	+20.6
1985	127.75	+51.9	+360.5	1546.67	+27.7	+54.0
1986	137.60	+7.7	+396.0	1895.95	+22.6	+88.7
1987	144.04	+4.7	+419.3	1938.83	+2.3	+93.0
1988	161.79	+12.3	+483.2	2168.57	+11.9	+115.9
1989	207.11	+28.0	+646.6	2753.20	+27.0	+174.1

YEAR	Good Money Utility Average			Dow Jones Utility Average		
		Change			Change	
	VALUE	FROM LAST YEAR	CUMULATIVE	VALUE	FROM LAST YEAR	CUMULATIVE
1976	22.89	—	—	108.38	—	—
1977	25.33	+10.7%	+10.7%	111.28	+2.7%	+2.7%
1978	21.45	−15.4	−6.3	98.24	−11.7	−9.4
1979	22.36	+4.2	−2.3	106.60	+8.5	−1.6
1980	23.46	+4.9	+2.5	114.42	+7.3	+5.6
1981	24.87	+6.0	+8.7	109.02	−4.7	+.6
1982	34.51	+38.8	+50.8	119.46	+9.6	+10.2
1983	45.34	+31.4	+98.1	131.80	+10.3	+21.6
1984	43.52	−4.0	+90.1	149.52	+13.5	+38.0
1985	51.74	+18.9	+126.0	174.81	+16.9	+61.3
1986	71.71	+38.6	+213.3	206.01	+17.5	+90.1
1987	63.44	−11.5	+177.2	175.08	−15.0	+61.5
1988	67.87	+7.0	+196.5	186.28	+6.4	+71.9
1989	74.54	+9.8	+225.6	235.04	+26.2	+116.9

year, while the DJUA had lost 15 percent of its value during that time. In 1988 the GMUA resumed its around 2.5-to-1 better long-term performance compared with the DJUA.

The comparison of GOOD MONEY's and the Dow's averages since 1976 also can be depicted visually, and, in so doing, the better performance of the socially screened average becomes even more evident.

What can be concluded from these comparisons? At the very least, they demonstrate that there is no inherent or unavoidable reason why investors should give up economic rewards while making social decisions in their investment choices. Nevertheless, GOOD MONEY's averages suffer the same limitations as any artificial average. They may not reflect what is actually going on in the "real world" of social investing. How, then, have the actual investments of social investors done over the years?

Performance of
GOOD MONEY STOCK AVERAGES
compared with
DOW JONES STOCK AVERAGES

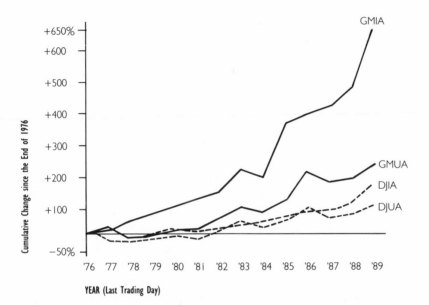

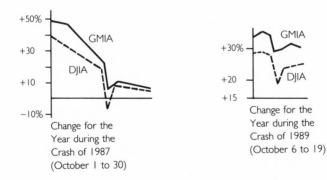

HOW SOCIAL INVESTORS HAVE FARED

In 1985 Ted Brown and Tom Van Dyck of Dean Witter Reynolds completed a study for the Africa Fund, which compared 124 companies that were "South Africa-free" to 124 that had South African connections. From the beginning of 1980 through 1984 the total return (capital gains plus dividends received) for the free portfolio was 20.75 percent, compared with 16.06 percent for the connected portfolio. In a more recent study the two financial analysts compared 105 free companies to 105 connected companies in the portfolio of the California Teachers and Employees Retirement System (the largest such fund in the country and one that employs a number of social screens). Return for the free group was 36.16 percent, compared with 20.18 percent for the connected group, for the previous four-year period.

At about the same time Peter Kinder, coauthor of a book on ethical investing, selected 400 socially responsible companies from a list of more than 1,000 large and small companies. He called his 400 the Social Index. From 1983 through 1988 an investor putting $1,000 into the index would have received a total gain (capital gains plus dividends received) of 164.7 percent while the same amount of money invested in the S&P 500 gained only 101.7 percent.

In 1989 Kinder joined with Steve Lydenberg and Amy Domini to form Kinder, Lydenberg, Domini & Co., Inc.—a company specializing in money management services for social investors. Lydenberg's index was refined and renamed the Domini Social Index (DSI). The DSI of 400 stocks was back-tested for fifty months beginning with January 1986. For that period of time the DSI had an average monthly gain of +1.36 percent compared with a monthly gain of +1.35 percent for the S&P 500. More significant, the DSI did better (went up more or down less than the S&P 500) in thirty-one of the fifty months, or 62 percent of the time.

By 1989 Modern Portfolio Theory Associates in New York City had been involved with South Africa-free investments for about two years. The investment management firm reported that during that time, through both bull and bear markets, its South African Free (SAFE) investments had performed well in comparison with the S&P 500:

YEAR	QUARTER	SAFE	S&P 500
1987	First	+23.90%	+21.30%
	Second	+2.70	+5.00
	Third	+7.00	+6.60
	Fourth	−23.50	−22.60
1988	First	+9.60	+5.70
	Second	+5.40	+6.50
	Third	+.60	+.33
	Fourth	+1.60	+3.00
For two years:		+23.03%	+22.23%

Perhaps the best available measure of the performance of socially screened portfolios can be found by comparing the performance of socially screened money funds with market averages. By mid-1990 there were more than thirty socially screened equity, bond, money market, and mutual funds available to the public in the United States (see Chapter 6 for a complete description of these funds). Some of the funds have single screens (for example, gold funds that screen only for South Africa), others have fairly weak social screens (avoidance of only alcohol, tobacco, and gambling companies), and still others have very demanding screens.

Some of the best-known socially screened funds are those managed by the Calvert Social Investment Fund in Washington, D.C. In 1985 Calvert offered investors nine money market funds and five mutual funds. During 1984 Calvert's socially screened money market fund was its third-best performer for that group, while its screened mutual fund was its leading performer for its group.

Also in 1985, the Council on Economic Priorities reported that the performance for some social funds for 1984 was especially strong and the social funds as a whole did as well as or slightly better than traditional funds. For the year, Lipper's General Equity Average (an average for 412 nonsocially screened mutual funds lost) 2.3 percent in value. In contrast, Calvert's Social Investment Fund rose 6.8 percent, Pax World Fund rose 6.5 percent, and New Alternatives Fund (screens for alternative and renewable energy) lost a small six-tenths of 1 percent. For 1984, Donogue's Money Fund Average (all nonscreened money market funds) rose 10.4 percent, and the average for fifty of the largest bank-offered (nonscreened) money market funds rose 9.28 percent. In contrast, Calvert led both these averages with a 10.21 percent gain. This was closely followed by Working Assets Money Fund (a number of different social screens) with a 9.99 percent rise.

In 1987 Kiplinger's published a *Financial Services Directory* that ranked 848 mutual funds identified by Lipper Analytical Services as being in existence for at least one year. At that time the industry average for performance over the prior year was +27.7 percent. Three of the best-known social funds had outperformed the industry average for the year: New Alternatives, +35.4 percent; Calvert, +32.9 percent; and Parnassus (a contrarian social fund that invests in out-of-favor companies), +29.0 percent. Two

CALVERT MONEY MARKET PORTFOLIO	1984 COMPOUNDED YIELD
Income	12.42%
T-Bill extra	10.50
Social investment	10.21
Plus prime	10.08
First variable rate	10.07
Tax-free: long-term	9.57
Government	9.32
Tax-free: limited-term	6.84
Tax-free: money market	5.98

CALVERT MUTUAL FUND PORTFOLIO	1984 NET ASSET VALUE CHANGE
Social investment	+6.8%
Income	+3.2
Tax-free: limited-term	+0.4
Tax-free: long-term	−1.7
Equity	−6.6

social funds underperformed the industry average. Pax World was slightly under the average with a gain of 25.2 percent, while Dreyfus Third Century (known for having one of the weakest social screens) finished the year with an 18.4 percent gain.

The real test for the screened funds, however, came during the crash of 1987. During this year the screened funds had to put their money where their mouths were. According to Lipper Analytical Services, nine of eleven screened mutual funds tracked over a one-year period prior to April 1988 outperformed or nearly equaled the averages of nonscreened funds. The week of the crash Calvert's $150 million Managed Growth Portfolio (screened mutual fund) dropped just 8 percent, compared with the almost 24 percent drop in the DJIA. Pax World's $67 million fund dipped just 8 percent from October 15 to October 30, compared with a 15 percent drop for the DJIA.

During the 1987 crash a relatively new social fund, started in late 1986, the Ariel Growth Fund, had an even more surprising performance. Ariel was designed by a privately held minority-owned money management house and is managed by Calvert. The fund screens for South Africa, companies primarily engaged in the manufacture of weapons systems, and companies producing nuclear energy or nuclear energy equipment. It looks for stable companies that have long and established records and exceptional long-term growth prospects. Lipper Analytical Services ranked Ariel as the number one small-company growth fund with assets under $25 million for 1987, despite the crash. Lipper also ranked Ariel number two for all small-company growth funds regardless of size.

What was going on? Writing in *Barron's* on how the do-good portfolios did better during the crash, Joseph Queenan put it this way: "[It's] almost as if they knew something the rest of us didn't know. Almost as if they'd gotten a message from above. A message saying 'Go ye forth and liquidate equities. Get thee hence and holdeth cash.' " *Newsweek* explained: "But the real reason the liberal funds have done well in the rocky market is that they tend to be so conservative. . . . [In addition] the stocks of the smaller, less speculative companies that these funds favor also tend to be less liquid, so they don't fluctuate much in rough markets."

During 1988 Lipper reported that growth funds did the best. The top ten funds nationally finished the year with an average gain of 42.44 percent, with Kaufman finishing first, at +58.57 percent, and Fidelity Capital Appreciation finishing tenth, at +37.62 percent. This compared with a gain for the Standard & Poor's 500 Index of 16.55 percent. Among the top ten growth funds were two with social screens: Parnassus with a year's gain of 42.44 percent and Ariel Growth with a gain of 39.97 percent.

Far from being a liberal, dreamy-eyed approach to investing, an approach that runs great economic risks and promotes bad investment decisions, SRI encourages precisely the opposite. The experience of the early 1987 bull market followed by a sharp drop indicates that social investors were far more likely to spot the speculative excesses of a runaway bull market than their traditional investment counterparts. Indeed, before October 19, 1987, Calvert's stock holdings had been pared from 76 percent of the fund's portfolio to 57 percent. Furthermore, social investors eschew short-term profits and look for long-term gains in stable, growing companies that provide badly needed goods and services. It is this economically conservative aspect of SRI that the traditional investment community and business press have yet to recognize.

In several ways, it is somewhat unfair to compare the performance of artificial market averages with the performance of managed funds, though it is done all the time in the financial press— and in this book. For purposes of making comparisons, some common base lines are required, and generally accepted stock averages, such as the Dow and Standard & Poor's, serve that purpose.

The unfairness in the comparison of averages with managed portfolios lies in the fact that the former constitutes arbitrary statistical devices while the latter involves financial accountability. Managers of funds have the fiduciary responsibility to protect and preserve the capital investments of others. As a consequence, they will frequently move their investments out of equities into fixed-income money instruments, especially in times of market instability. By so doing, they sacrifice potential capital gains in favor of financial security. In addition, fund managers must reflect the special preferences and interests of their clients, which may place restrictions on investment opportunities.

In contrast, those who design and track averages (such as GOOD MONEY Publications and Dow Jones) have nothing to lose if an average goes up or down. Averages are merely educational or testing devices, and designers are free to reflect whatever they are attempting to measure in any way they please. In this sense, even comparing averages to other averages is risky. The GMIA, which contains industry groups not included in the Dow, is a better representation of the overall U.S. economy than the DJIA. The DJIA sticks with the larger companies, largely ignores new companies with high-growth potential, and reflects the economically troubled aspects of smokestack America (for example, the steel industry). It is not surprising, then, that the GMIA has done far better than the DJIA over the long term.

The most valid comparisons, ones stressed in this book, are how socially screened funds perform compared with funds without social screens or how socially responsible companies perform compared with companies with bad social records. Those comparisons suggest that at the least, socially concerned investors and businesspeople will do as well as everyone else. Moreover, with a little bit of luck (which is needed in all kinds of investing), social investors and businesspeople will do a great deal better economically.

3

THE GOALS OF
SOCIAL INVESTING

The various strategies employed by ethically and socially concerned investors and businesspeople are designed to respond to a number of different social problems and issues. However, four general goals may be identified. First, SRI involves strategies to democratize the economy in two important ways: encouragement of the hiring, retention, and promotion of women and minorities and the increase of worker ownership in corporate America. Second, recognizing the human price that has been paid in the workplace for much industrial development, SRI promotes practices to humanize the work environment. These include alternatives to the traditional assembly line and the promotion of a clean, safe, and rewarding work environment. These two goals must be achieved within the context of making a profit. However, profit may be misused for unsafe and exploitive purposes, and ironically, this can have a serious and negative economic impact. Therefore, a third goal of SRI involves rethinking the ways profit has been traditionally used and distributed. Finally, all these goals are related to a fourth goal: convincing the business world that a corporate conscience can pay.

DEMOCRATIZING THE ECONOMY

The contemporary economy has become one of the least demo-cratic and least egalitarian contexts within which people live, despite the importance America places upon these values. Wealth has steadily been concentrated in fewer and fewer hands. A mere 10 percent of American households own close to 90 percent of all financial assets, including stocks, bonds, savings, property, and the like. Similarly, there has been an increasing concentra-tion of stock ownership. Only 20 percent of U.S. families own stock, and fewer than 6 percent own fifty thousand dollars or more in stock. When one adds privately held stock, the picture becomes even bleaker, with a mere 2 percent owning more than half of all private stock. Such an uneven concentration of wealth leads to two results: Increasing numbers of citizens fall farther behind economically, and much wealth is unavailable to help resolve major social problems.

A 1988 *Fortune* magazine report concluded that gains for Afri-can-Americans in business had been poor to dismal since the civil rights movement push for equality started more than twenty years earlier. There has been a growing black middle class in America, consisting of physicians, lawyers, other professionals, military officers, entrepreneurs, and state and city officials. How-ever, by the end of 1987 only one African-American headed a *Fortune* 1,000 company: Clifton Wharton, Jr., chairman and chief executive officer of the Teachers Insurance and Annuity Association. Jerry Williams was the heir apparent to AM Inter-national, a large graphics company that was number 390 on the *Fortune* Industrials 500 list. African-Americans make up about 12 percent of the U.S. population. If there were equitable distri-bution and equal opportunity in the marketplace, one would expect to find about 120 and 60 black CEOs, respectively, on those two lists. Also cited in *Fortune's* report was information from the country's leading business schools. At MIT's Sloan School, Stan-ford University, and the University of Chicago, African-American M.B.A.'s constituted between 3 and 4 percent of the 1987 graduating class. At Columbia, Harvard, the University of Michigan, and Wharton, the number of African-Americans increased slightly from 1982, but they still made up fewer than 7 percent of the 1987 M.B.A. class.

What this lack of black participation in the upper echelons of corporate America means is that needed human resources are being wasted at a time when the U.S. economy can ill afford such a waste. For example, IBM's CEO John Akers explained to *Fortune* magazine that he felt so strongly about the need for affirmative action that he sent a telegram to White House Chief of Staff Donald Regan pointing out that his company would remain committed to the policy regardless of the Reagan administration's position. What IBM did was follow a policy that involved careful planning and coordination. This was based upon an analysis of how people obtained key jobs. If a future black branch manager was going to be needed, it was necessary to hire ten black salespeople from whom the future selection could be made.

In early 1989 Chairman James R. Houghton of Corning told the *Wall Street Journal:* "We do a good job at hiring [blacks and women] but a lousy job at retention and promotion. And it's not good enough just to bring them through the front door." From 1980 to 1987 the company lost one in six African-American professionals and one in seven female professionals, compared with one in fourteen white male professionals. This represented not only a loss of talent for Corning but also a loss in the cost of hiring and training black and women professionals.

Houghton told Corning's white male managers that their own promotions would depend upon how well they helped women and minorities achieve their fullest potential. To the company's already existing benefits (which included child care, maternity leave, and flextime) programs and practices were added in order to increase significantly the number of minorities among top senior managers as quickly as possible. These included:

Job rotation about every year and a half for newly employed blacks so that they could have exposure to a full range of job experiences

Lifting limits on personnel so that managers could hire talented minorities when they spotted them

Participation in regional African-American and women's professional organizations and sponsorship of events

Sponsorship of several-day workshops for small groups of managers at which black and female managers could share their views about sexism and racism

Since Corning is located in rural western New York, its aggressive affirmative action program faces special difficulties. Small-town life does not appeal to many minorities. The local community does not provide many of the social networks, services, and support groups that minority residents like and require. As a result, Corning began a program to attract minority businesses to the area.

The philosophy of SRI would argue that sexism and racism are ethical failures in two ways. From a utilitarian standpoint, they are practices that waste human resources, a waste that American corporations cannot afford. Robert Beck, a white executive vice-president at BankAmerica, told *Fortune* magazine: "[Getting more African-Americans into business] is not a social issue or a moral issue—it's a business priority." A. Barry Rand, president of Xerox USA, the Xerox Corporation's sales and service division, commented: "The U.S. is in a global trade war and we're trying to fight without all our troops." Just as important, however, is that, from a moral standpoint, sexism and racism erode the values of freedom, equality, and human dignity. A society without these values reflected in its economic life is a society that is spiritually and morally bankrupt.

Nowhere is the goal of democratizing the economy better reflected than in the growth and spread of employee stock ownership plans. As Corey Rosen, director of the National Center for Employee Ownership (NCEO), has pointed out, the idea of redistributing wealth through plans whereby employees can purchase shares of stock in the companies they work for is not new. However, the popularity of employee stock ownership plans (ESOPs) has spread rapidly in only the last several decades.

In 1975 there were 1,601 ESOPs involving 248,000 employees. By 1978 those figures had increased dramatically to 4,028 plans and 2.8 million employees. One decade later there were 9,407 ESOPs covering more than 9.6 million employees. About 90 percent of the plans were in private companies. More than half the private company plans owned 30 percent or more of the company's stock, and about a third owned a majority.

In the 1950s investment banker Louis Kelso argued that everyone should own productive capital in order to build a personal capital estate, foster economic democracy, and create widespread support for capitalism. For several decades he developed the idea of ESOPs in his writing and research. In the 1970s he met with Senator Russell Long, the son of Louisiana's well-known populist governor Huey Long. Russell Long was able to get the U.S. Congress to approve a number of bills that gave corporations strong tax incentives to initiate ESOPs. Corey Rosen quotes Long as saying that the idea was like "Huey Long without the Robin Hood."

For example, in 1972 the Chicago and North Western Railroad was owned by a parent company that wanted out of the railroad business. C&NW management resisted the idea of selling the railroad to another conglomerate, and it didn't want to try to save the company by incurring substantial debt through loans from the financial community.

As an alternative, up to 300,000 shares of new stock (the stock was publicly traded on the New York Stock Exchange) were offered to employees at $50 a share, with a minimum purchase of $500 and a maximum of $100,000. About 1,000 of the 13,000 C&NW employees bought over 72,000 shares of stock, raising $3.6 million in equity capital. However, this was not merely a way of raising internal capital free from outside influence. Railroading requires small teams working together without supervision and, therefore, is especially amenable to the idea of employee ownership and participation in management decision making.

So successful was the original plan that after a sixty-for-one stock split in 1974, the company set up an ESOP through which all employees could purchase stock by means of a payroll deduction plan. It created a new company spirit that led to the modernization of tracks, trains running faster, and new employee training programs—all at a time when most U.S. railroads were going bankrupt. By 1982 a minimum $500 initial purchase of 10 shares in 1972 had grown to 1,800 shares worth about $36,000, a gain of 7,200 percent. By that time those employees who had bought the maximum of 2,000 shares for $100,000 ten years earlier had 360,000 shares worth more than $7 million.

In 1983 NCEO reported that the country's largest sugar company, U.S. Sugar, had set up an ESOP to permit employees to purchase stock held by the Charles Stewart Mott family. The plan was designed to encourage workers to own about 47 percent of the company. By 1986 NCEO listed sixty-six companies with major ESOPs. Fifteen of these had 100 percent employee ownership and included Denver Yellow Cab, Publix Supermarkets, and Weirton Steel—among the best-known stories of employee ownership. Other companies included some of the country's largest and most successful: Federal Express, FMC Corporation, Katz Communications, Lowe's Companies, Ashland Oil, and Herman Miller. In 1987 NCEO announced that more than half a million employees had been added to ESOPs during the previous year, and two of the largest buy-ups in history, involving the Hospital Corporation of America and United Airlines, were in the works. W. W. Norton & Company, the publisher of this book, is an employee-owned company.

ESOPs are not always beneficial or well intentioned. In a 1987 *Business Week* column Robert Kuttner documented instances in which ESOPs were set up by managements to dump unprofitable parts of businesses on unsuspecting employees. According to Kuttner, the Hospital Corporation of America's management used an ESOP to sell off 104 specialty hospitals because they were low-profit generators, compared with the company's high-profit general hospitals. In the case of United Airlines, Kuttner argued that management wanted to sell off hotel and car rental businesses, persuade employees to take big pay cuts in exchange for a minority ownership, and use the money gained by the ESOP to offer sufficient shareholder bonuses in order to maintain control of the company.

There is no question that Kuttner's criticism of some ESOPs is warranted, and these problems have been examined in detail in a recent book by Joseph R. Blasi, *Employee Ownership: Revolution or Ripoff?* In spite of these examples, research discloses that in many cases ESOPs lead to important financial and social gains. A 1978 NCEO study found that a sample of employee ownership companies were one and one-half times as profitable as comparable non-ESOP companies. A 1980 study by the same organization disclosed that employee-owned companies with ESOPs had twice the average annual productivity growth rate. In 1983 a study discovered that companies in which a majority of the employees owned a majority of stock generated three times more net jobs than comparable non-ESOP firms. A study in 1984 found that thirteen publicly traded companies with at least 10 percent employee ownership outperformed from 62 to 75 percent of their competitors by various measures of company performance.

Finally, a 1984 NCEO study disclosed, for the first time, a causal link between employee ownership and corporate performance. The study involved 283 companies—45 ESOP companies each matched to 5 or more similar non-ESOP companies. Performance data were collected for 1970 to 1985. As a result, pre-ESOP and post-ESOP comparisons could be made for the companies that went through this transition during this period. In terms of employment, ESOP companies grew 5.05 percent per year faster than their competitors after ESOPs had been established, compared with only 1.21 percent per year faster before their ESOPs. In terms of sales, ESOP companies grew 5.40 percent faster after their ESOPs, compared with only 1.89 percent per year faster before.

Corporate productivity and profitability are, obviously, the result of many different factors. Employee ownership is not an automatic panacea for all corporate problems, but used properly, ESOPs can result in increased employee pride and commitment.

HUMANIZING THE WORKPLACE

As important as democratizing the economy is humanizing the workplace—another opportunity for businesses to increase productivity (and thus profits) while simultaneously improving the lives of workers. However, the issue is far more complex than merely problems of workplace health and safety. The psychological component is critical. Many workplaces require passive, rather than participatory, involvement on the part of workers. As many businesses have recently discovered, this can lead to high rates of employee absenteeism, low productivity, and lax worker on-job performance and, in turn, to falling revenues, poor and dangerous products and services, and degradation of the quality of work life as a whole. Since we spend most of our waking hours at our jobs, this situation constitutes a major problem. Furthermore, one of the early promises of industrial capitalism was the liberation of citizens from demeaning and unsafe labor. This promise has often not been realized.

One movement to democratize and to humanize the workplace is what is known as worker participation or employee involvement (jointness, as it is sometimes called). This involves both management and employees working in teams to reach joint decisions. In a major 1989 feature story *Business Week* pointed out that there is still much resistance to worker participation in U.S. industries since some executives are fearful of losing control and some labor leaders see it as a way of co-opting workers to increase productivity artificially. However, a growing number of large American corporations have begun to utilize self-managed work-teams, finding they are good for employee morale and for the bottom line. *Business Week* listed the following companies, which collectively employed almost two million workers and had more than $300 billion in 1988 revenues, as examples of ones employing work teams:

For 1988

COMPANY	NUMBER OF EMPLOYEES	REVENUES (MILLION)	WHEN STARTED
General Motors	766,000	$120,388	1975
Ford Motor	358,900	92,446	1982
General Electric	298,000	38,824	1985
Boeing	154,000	16,962	1987
Digital Equipment	125,400	9,390	1982
Procter & Gamble	77,000	19,336	1962
Caterpillar	60,560	10,435	1986
LTV Corporation	39,000	7,325	1985
Champion International	30,400	5,129	1985
Cummins Engine	26,100	3,310	1973
Tektronix	16,085	1,412	1983
A. O. Smith	11,500	1,015	1987

As this table indicates, the concept of teamwork was popular early in the automotive industry.

One of the most remarkable and successful examples of a major attempt to humanize the workplace is found in the Saab and Volvo automobile plants in Sweden. The automobile industry, with its assembly lines, has long been known for its boring and repetitious work. Workers and equipment are grouped so that work continually passes from one operation to the next in a straight line. The assembly line always moves and, more important, can be sped up by management in order to increase productivity artificially. What usually results is decreased worker safety and product quality. Several decades ago the Saab and Volvo management decided to scrap the assembly line in favor of an alternative way of building automobiles. With cooperation and advice from the Swedish socialist government, strong labor unions, and the Scandinavian Institutes for Administrative Research, management rethought the entire process by which autos had been traditionally manufactured.

The Volvo automobile company was founded in 1927 and, by 1990, employed 78,614 people, more than 20 percent of them women found at all job levels. The company's 1989 revenues were almost $15 billion. One of the main assembly plants is located in Volvo City, on the outskirts of Göteborg. The community has a post office, various businesses and services, and a leisure center with sauna, to which all employees have access. Symbolic of the company's desire to involve workers in decision making, when construction was started on a fifth assembly plant, Volvo picked workers from other plants to test new ideas for the assembly process.

Special care has been taken to provide the cleanest and most noise-free work environment. In the area of the stamping presses in the Göteborg plant, where the fender, hood, roof, and other body parts are formed, Volvo went to the expense of replacing the usual concrete floor with thousands of inch-square stakes pounded into the ground. These wooden stakes absorb noise so that it is possible to stand by the presses and talk in whispers.

Hydraulic robots are used throughout the factory to minimize other noise. Savings through automation and robotics go into training programs for all employees, especially younger workers, thereby avoiding the problem of job displacement. Technology is used to ease work, and very little human bending, squatting, or crawling is required during the entire process of assembling an automobile. Automated arms can lift auto bodies and tip them over for easier access to needed work, and they are used to transport heavy and dangerous auto parts. This automation also increases quality control by making a complete inspection of all units easier and more thorough. Volvo purchases Swedish robots in order to help the national economy. Robots are also used for painting and dipping auto body parts, making human exposure to fumes unnecessary, and robots do 99 percent of all spot welds, after which employees are used for meticulous quality control inspection. Any inadequate welds can be corrected by hand.

The most striking feature of Volvo's Göteborg plant is the complete absence of the typical assembly-line technology. The key concept is teamwork. This is made possible by slowly moving platforms upon which rest various body, engine, and other units to be assembled. As a team of workers completes the job atop each platform, the platform slowly moves on magnetic tracks to another step in the assembly process within the plant. Workers can, as a team, decide who works on which aspect of the unit assembly process, and employees are frequently changed from one assembly team station to another, thereby obtaining additional skills. Every team work space has a rest and meeting area. In addition, since there is no assembly line, the assembly process can be stopped at any time to check for quality controls.

In 1988 Volvo came up with a better idea for marrying the company's need to make a profit with a concern for the interests of its customers. In conjunction with Chase Manhattan the company offered ten-year auto loans—the longest in the industry. Though the buyer had to put down a sizable 25 percent payment in order to qualify, the length of the loan dropped monthly payments to almost half. The policy was designed to make Volvo's expensive upscale cars more available to cost-conscious customers. Such long loans are anathema to some automakers since many cars are not designed to last as long as ten years. The longest loan offered by General Motors' credit division in 1988 was five years, although the company was considering six- or seven-year loans because of increasing competition from some banks and the Volvo policy. Is there a risk that long loans will outlast the life of an automobile and thereby contribute to a higher rate of defaults? By 1989 GM had announced that it had had to repossess more than 150,000 autos sold on credit because owners simply stopped paying as the resale / turn-in value plummeted in a few short years so that the cars' values were less than the remaining costs of the outstanding loans. However, Volvo's cars are built and guaranteed to last, under normal driving conditions, for exceptionally long periods of time and mileage.

The profitability factor associated with Volvo's extraordinary social programs for workers has been exceptional. The company began its restructuring of the workplace in the 1970s. At that time, by almost any measure, the company was not doing well and its overall performance was dropping. However, by the late 1970s that situation had turned around suddenly, and as the following figures demonstrate, Volvo's performance (and return to investors) have been excellent:

	1973 TO 1977	1977 TO 1988
Average yearly ADR* price	−64%	+699%
Earnings per ADR	−59	+848
Dividends declared per ADR	+15	+332

*Since Volvo is a foreign company, its stock is sold on the New York Stock Exchange as American depository receipts [ADRs]. See Chapter 8.

MAKING A CORPORATE CONSCIENCE PAY OFF

Marrying corporate social consciences and profitability is not always an easy task but it is not impossible. The biggest difficulty is that it takes a very different perspective about business practices and the uses of profits than that usually taught in business schools. The usual view was summarized in a statement by former General Motors Chairman Thomas Murphy: "General Motors is not in the business of making cars. It is in the business of making money." A contrasting view was expressed by financial adviser Eliot Janeway: "[W]hy does money have the potential to destroy your life? Why does money make so many people unhappy; it's because too few of us understand how to use it properly to let it give us freedom. Money is only a means to an end, not an end in itself." That is the substance of the problem in the modern economy. Bigger profits have become an end in themselves, rather than a means to produce good products and services, create jobs for a vibrant economy, and improve the general quality of life for oneself and others.

One of the most striking examples of the different view are Ben Cohen and Jerry Greenfield of Ben & Jerry's Homemade Inc. In 1978 Ben & Jerry's began making ice cream in an abandoned gasoline station in Burlington, Vermont. By the end of 1989 the company was selling more than $58 million worth of ice cream in supermarkets in forty-two states and from 90 franchises, earning more than $2 million in profits. In Boston, Ben & Jerry's sold

50 percent of all high-price ice cream. However, from the start Ben & Jerry's had more than profitability in mind.

The company funds progressive causes, including donating 7.5 percent of its profits to charitable causes, of which 1 percent goes to a peace organization, far more than most other corporations. By the end of 1989 Ben Cohen had started another company that makes nut brittle (candy) out of nuts harvested from the threatened Brazilian rain forest. The company planned to buy 150,000 pounds of nuts a year and give 40 percent of the profits to organizations working to protect the rain forest. In addition, since the new company planned to purchase Brazil and cashew nuts directly from the growers, it could pay them three to ten times more than the usual market price because the arrangement eliminated the middleman.

In an interview for the *Boston Globe*, Ben Cohen explained his philosophy of business as follows: "My belief is that it is in the business environment that you have the most opportunity to act on [your] values. It is when we are in the business environment that we are most powerful, that we have the most potential to effect social change." According to Tom Peters, coauthor of *In Search of Excellence*, one of the changes so badly needed is a major restructuring of U.S. corporations, particularly in the way in which top executives reward themselves in pay, bonuses, and other perks: "The executive-compensation system has no coherence, makes no sense, and, at a time when there's a requirement for violent restructuring in companies, has a very negative impact."

At financially successful Ben & Jerry's, Ben Cohen took home only $60,961 plus a $10,000 bonus in 1987, an amount significantly lower than the typical pay for top executives. *Business Week* analyzed the total pay and compensation for the CEOs of 355 companies in thirty-six industry areas for 1989. The average compensation was well over $1 million for the year. The magazine also measured total pay against three-year return to shareholders and three-year profits and found that in a large number of cases there was no correlation. For example, C. O. McCaw of McCaw Cellular took home $54 million for the year, though his company had never made a profit. Steven T. Ross of Time Warner took home $34 million, though his company had a loss for the year and company debt increased substantially because of a merger of Time and Warner. Paul Fireman of Reebok International and Martin S. Davis of Paramount took home $15 million and $12 million respectively, although their companies received *Business Week*'s lowest rating for correlation between total pay and corporate performance.

In contrast, at Ben & Jerry's there is a ratio of seven to one between the highest-paid and the lowest-paying positions. In other words, if the boss wants a raise, everyone else gets a proportionate raise. And everyone at Ben & Jerry's knows what the boss makes. It is obvious that this policy has not impeded Ben Cohen's ability to be an effective CEO, nor has it impeded Ben & Jerry's ability to compete successfully in a for-profit economy. Though this compensation policy is extremely unusual, it is not an exception. In the 1970s the insurance company IGP (International Group Plans) of Washington, D.C., had a similar ratio. Retail store operator Dayton Hudson uses a twenty to one ratio.

The philosophy of companies with pay scales was expressed in the following jingle by eighteenth-century satirist Jonathan Swift:

> Money, the life-blood of the nation,
> > Corrupts and stagnates in the veins,
> Unless a proper circulation
> > Its motion and its heat maintains.

Socially, for-profit practices should be a way in which economic resources are channeled so that they can be used to resolve some of the world's most pressing problems. The central tenet of SRI is that making money and doing social good can go hand in hand since they are mutually self-sustaining. In his company's 1983 *Annual Report* Corning's Chairman James Houghton put it this way: "It's easy to be cynical. It's tempting to reach for the passing short-term gain of a patent infringement, a callous treatment of employees, an indifference to the community where you're located, an exploitive deal with a customer in urgent need of your product. Long term, it's a net loss. It results in the creative executive who goes elsewhere, the lathe operator who works listlessly, the customer whose door is closed the next time you visit."

For about a decade Johnson & Johnson has been selling a "wellness" program to its employees. The goals of the program are to persuade employees to stop smoking, eat more fruit and fewer fatty foods, get more exercise, and buckle up their seat belts. The company decided to conduct a three-year study to determine what the costs of its wellness program were. The study found that though health care costs at J&J (which is self-insured) had risen 310 percent in a decade, costs had jumped an estimated 460 percent at thirty similar companies that J&J tracks to determine its own wage and compensation levels. In 1989 J&J saved $378 per employee through lower absenteeism and the slower rise in the company's health care expenses.

RESPONSIBLE COMPANIES DO BETTER

One strong measure of a corporation's sense of social responsibility is how its executives respond in the case of product or service disasters—either of their own making or by accident. These cases also provide the opportunity to measure whether or not a socially concerned response is profitable. There have been several examples of exceptional corporate response in recent years, which can be compared with well-known cases of corporate irresponsibility.

When two young children died from strangulation while swallowing parts of Parker Brothers' highly successful Riviton toy, its parent company, General Mills, did not hesitate to support the decision to withdraw the toy sets at a cost of about $10 million. News releases about the dangers were sent to all wire services, and an extra public relations officer was hired to ensure adequate consumer-directed publicity for the recall. When queried by the press about this unusually responsible corporate behavior, Parker Brothers' president replied: "What were we supposed to do? Wait for the third child to die?"

One of the most well-known and exceptional cases of recent corporate responsibility was the action taken by Johnson & Johnson after the discovery that samples of its leading product and profit maker Tylenol had been tainted with cyanide. Instead of covering up the problem or accusing the media of overplaying the poisonings, J&J asked consumers to remove the product from home medicine cabinets and stores to remove it from their shelves and return it for a refund. Chief Executive Officer James Burke appeared on national television to warn consumers of the danger. After a consumer death in early 1986, the company voluntarily replaced all Tylenol capsules with caplets, a product that is far more resistant to tampering. In addition, J&J designed packaging that was triple-wrapped to be tamperproof, something the pharmaceutical industry had resisted for years. This action defied traditional business logic, which dictated that talking about product disasters in public destroys consumer confidence and encourages lawsuits.

Nor is social responsibility confined to U.S. corporations. In 1985 a Japan Air Lines plane crash claimed 520 victims. JAL President Yasumoto Takagi immediately offered condolences, in person, to the relatives of the victims. He stood at the foot of the airplane ramp and bowed low as the relatives arrived in Tokyo. Then he announced he would resign as a reflection of his sense of full responsibility for the crash. This incident stands in stark contrast with Exxon's CEO Lawrence G. Rawl, who took some ten days to respond publicly to the disastrous oil spill in Valdez, Alaska. Then the response was in the form of a weak apology in a letter to the public that appeared in major newspapers. Rawl also steadfastly refused to go to Alaska, arguing that he didn't know how to clean up the spill and he would only get in the way.

A number of studies indicate that if done conscientiously, corporate responsibility during product disasters can be rewarded while corporate nonresponsibility can be costly. The J&J case probably offers the clearest proof of this conclusion. After Tylenol was withdrawn from the market and the capsules were replaced with caplets, many financial analysts predicted serious revenue drops for the company. To be sure, Tylenol's share of the pain-killer market dropped from about 35 to 20 percent immediately after the public disclosure of the poisonings. However, by mid-1986 the market share for Tylenol had rebounded to more than 30 percent.

Furthermore, J&J continued to develop and sell other products successfully and wasn't forced to deal with large lawsuits or compulsory government regulation. In 1981, the year before and during the poisonings, J&J's total sales were $5.4 billion and the company's net profit was $468 million. In the following year of 1982, sales increased to $5.8 billion and net profit to $523 million. By the end of 1988 sales had soared to more than $8 billion, and net profit had almost doubled to more than $900 million. The economic news for investors was also good. In 1981 J&J declared 42.5 cents in dividends and the stock sold for an average yearly price (high plus low divided by 2), of $34 per share. In 1982 J&J declared 49.5 cents per share in dividends and the stock sold for an average price of $42 per share. By the end of 1988 J&J's stock sold for more than $42 per share, and during the year 80.5 cents per share in dividends were paid. (NOTE: Throughout this book, when stock information is provided from year to year, it is adjusted for any later stock splits or dividends, so that figures over time will be comparable.)

Similarly, the Riviton crisis, which was managed with public honesty and integrity, appeared to have no impact upon the performance of General Mills, the parent company of Parker Brothers. From 1977, before the crisis, to 1981, shortly after the crisis, General Mills' earnings per share increased by 65 percent. The average yearly stock price increased by 6 percent for the same period of time, while dividends declared per share jumped 82 percent.

In 1983 GOOD MONEY Publications studied the short-term performance of five companies that had been involved in well-publicized and mismanaged product disasters. When Firestone Tire & Rubber's 500-radial tires started disintegrating and causing highway deaths and injuries, management blamed consumer misuse of the product. The company hired actor Jimmy Stewart to produce television advertisements that reminded consumers that it still had the same concern for quality as the company founder, "good old Harvey Firestone." When Ford Motor's Pinto was found to have a fatal exhaust system that caused the gas tank to explode in rear-end collisions, management falsely claimed no prior knowledge of the flawed design. Indeed, it later became known that Ford had priced the possible legal expenses of deaths and injuries and had decided that these would require less cost than would be involved in changing the design of the automobile.

When Ralph Nader wrote that General Motors' Corvair was "unsafe at any speed" and tended to flip over in low-speed turns, the company responded by hiring a private detective to investigate Nader's private life. When workers sued the Manville Corporation after contracting the lung disease asbestosis, management said it didn't know about the dangers in spite of an industry-sponsored study by the Metropolitan Life Insurance Company that, as early as 1929, had identified asbestos-related health hazards. After the accident at the Three Mile Island nuclear power plant, General Public Utilities' management attempted to downgrade concerns and manipulate public opinion, and this did more damage to public confidence than the original incident.

As the accompanying table shows, the performance for these five companies was far better before the mishandled incidents than immediately after. In addition, Manville eventually declared bankruptcy in order to reorganize its financial affairs. By 1989 the company had emerged from reorganization and was still alive. However, it faced severe problems, including a damaged reputation and big annual payments to a court-created trust for asbestos

	Years		Change In		
COMPANY	BEFORE/ DURING DISASTER	AFTER DISASTER	AVERAGE YEARLY STOCK PRICE	DIVIDENDS DECLARED PER SHARE	EARNINGS PER SHARE
Firestone	1977	1979	−45%	−11%	−30%
Ford	1976	1981	−50	−46	−205
General Motors	1963	1970	−5	−15	−62
General Public Utilities	1978	1980	−63	−100	−85
Manville	1980	1982	−76	−65	−120
AVERAGE FOR FIVE COMPANIES:			−36%	−43%	−127%

victims. In the first half of 1990 Manville's stock began a steady
and unrelenting decline. To these cases can be added the story
of A. H. Robins Company and its Dalkon Shield birth control
device. From March 8, 1971, to June 28, 1974, Robins marketed
the intrauterine contraceptive device. When the public press began
to report injuries to users, including spontaneous abortions among
women who became pregnant despite using the shield, Robins's
common stock plunged from a high of more than $40 per share
to a low of about $8.

By the end of 1984 Robins and its insurer had already paid
more than $300 million in settlements of more than 8,000 law-
suits and about 4,000 additional claims remained unsettled. The
company established a $615 million fund to pay for additional
claims, and a separate fund was set up to pay almost $7 million
in claims from stockholders who had purchased the stock during
the time the shield was on the market. The shareholders charged
that Robins had known about the shield's dangers before it was
marketed and had done nothing. In 1985 Robins declared bankruptcy.

What these examples indicate is that socially irresponsible
companies are likely to run into severe economic problems in the
long run. In contrast, socially responsible companies will most
likely be profitably rewarded by approving customers and an
appreciative public.

4

IDENTIFYING RESPONSIBLE CORPORATIONS

Are there any corporate saints? Obviously not. However, the question typifies a concern that sometimes bedevils both people involved with SRI and observers of the movement. Just how can anyone use social or ethical values in making investment and business decisions when those values are difficult to measure, often elusive, and they change from one group to another? Furthermore, "sin" is an ever-present aspect of daily life, and no individual, organization, or society is without it—with the possible exception of Mother Teresa.

In 1986, writing about SRI in the *New England Monthly*, John Rothchild put it this way: "As profitable as ethical investing has been of late, there is no way, regrettably, to determine what it is, nor are there enough hours in the day for the noble futility of all these [ethical] distinctions. As sensible as this path appears for the first one or two steps, the end, I fear, is madness, or perhaps a more horrifying prospect: giving away all one's money." What is puzzling about Rothchild's comment is that even though he admits SRI has been economically profitable, he still rejects it. In a 1989 article for *Financial World*, Sana Siwolop concluded that ethical and social investing boils down to a lot of judgment calls since ethics are in the eye of the beholder.

There is some truth in such observations. Making ethical choices is never easy. Some ethical values do vary from group to group and person to person. However, to conclude that SRI is impossible or will lead to "madness" ignores a number of important things. Arguing that we should abandon ethical decisions in business and investments is a bit like arguing that we should give up the principles set forth in the Constitution of the United States because there is no such thing as an honest politician and the idea of human liberty is subject to multiple interpretations. What is seen as a weakness by the skeptics is actually one of the strengths of SRI—a healthy and vigorous debate about what constitutes ethical and socially responsible economic behavior.

Furthermore, the skepticism persists because of a number of unexamined assumptions about traditional investing, the place of ethical decision making in the investment process, and real-life corporate programs and practices. These assumptions include the following:

> While SRI is based upon highly personal and impossible-to-measure information, traditional investing is based upon easy-to-measure and factual information.
>
> There is no model or strategy available for making social judgments about investment decisions, whereas time-tested models exist for traditional investing.
>
> There are no such things as universal ethical standards or perfection in the corporate world. Therefore, the socially good companies cannot really be distinguished from the socially bad companies in most cases.

In fact, making ethical and social judgments in the investment process is no more difficult than making purely financial judgments.

LOOKING FOR THE BEST OF INDUSTRY

The president of a New York City investment firm put his finger on part of the problem in a 1982 interview about SRI with the *Futurist* magazine. He stated that social investing is irresponsible and used the following example: "Cement works are the worst polluters around. But would you say there should be no cement? No roads? No buildings?" The problem with this type of response is that it ducks the really important questions. Do cement works have to pollute, or can the pollution be controlled? If pollution controls are limited, can cement works be located where they do less environmental damage? Are there future alternatives to cement that could be researched and produced?

For example, coal mining was once considered the most dangerous occupation, and miners worked sixty hours per week. Then the United Mine Workers Union, the U.S. Bureau of Mines, some mineowners and miners began to develop and implement safety technologies and procedures, and the workweek dropped to thirty-five hours. With the discovery of acid rain, some utilities, such as Louisville Gas & Electric (recently renamed LG&E Energy) and Southwestern Public Service, have adopted state-of-the-art pollution control procedures, and others, such as Hawaiian Electric Industries and New England Electric System, are developing alternative energy technologies. As a consequence, investors can select those companies in an industry that contain or productively respond to the environmental and other social costs involved in using modern technology. They can seek out the best of the industry in terms of social record. A humorous example of this strategy was illustrated in a *Futurist* magazine article that quoted a dialogue between a bank trust officer and a socially concerned investor about what it means to make profitable investments in order to bring about positive social change:

"Investing is *solely* for profit," the trust officer exclaimed. "Hell, I'd invest in a whorehouse if it was legal—as in parts of Nevada—and it made money."

The investor thought for a moment and then replied: "Maybe I would, too, if the whorehouse was worker-owned or a cooperative."

A person looking for companies with the best social records within an industry is no different from a profit-only investor looking for those companies with the best financial records and prospects for the future. Since all business and industrial activity involves some kinds of social risks (potential harm to the environment, difficult working conditions, etc.), the challenge is to identify those corporations that try harder to deal with these risks. Consider the case of the McDonald's Corporation.

In 1954 Ray Kroc, the founder of McD's, opened his first restaurant in Illinois, with the motto Q, S, C & V (quality, service, cleanliness, and value). McD's outlets rapidly became known as safe and clean places to take the kids for an inexpensive meal. McD's also has a record for involvement in local community campaigns to encourage such things as fire prevention, bicycle safety, and litter cleanup. The famous Ronald McDonald Houses provide accommodations for families with children being treated for illnesses at nearby hospitals. By 1985 there were seventy-three such houses. Also in 1985, the company did not hesitate to close a California outlet and convert it into a public park following the massacre of customers by a crazed gunman. In 1984 McD's raised $200,000 to contribute to the United Negro College Fund, increasing its total donations from 1980 to 1984 to $600,000. In 1988 the company made voter registration cards available in a national campaign by some corporations to encourage more Americans to vote in the presidential election.

In their 1984 study of *The 100 Best Companies to Work for in America*, Robert Levering, Milton Moskowitz, and Michael Katz reported that McD's had a strong array of employee benefit programs, including profit sharing, an investment savings plan, and free physical examinations every other year for those under thirty-five years of age and every year for those over thirty-five. Around fifty employees were annually recognized for outstanding achievements, and they received an award that included a cash bonus equal to one-third of pay. In 1986 *USA Today* reported that McD's grants ten-week paid leave plus vacation to employees after ten years of service. Too, one does not need an M.B.A. degree to work for the company, and it is possible for employees to work their way from back of the counter up to president of the company.

In 1990 McDonald's decided to phase out the use of Styrofoam containers used for its fast-food products, in response to a letter from Vermont's Republican Senator Robert Stafford, which cited growing scientific evidence that foam packaging made from chlorofluorocarbons (CFCs) is environmentally dangerous. CFCs float upward and contribute to the destruction of the earth's stratospheric ozone layer, which shields humans from the sun's cancer-causing ultraviolet rays. McD's told Stafford that its earlier decision to switch from paper to foam packaging had been made partly as a result of concern for the destruction of forests. In late 1989 the company also began the recycling of paper products at its outlets. In late 1990 the company entered into a six-month consultation process with the Environmental Defense Fund that could transform McD's solid waste policies.

Though during his lifetime Ray Kroc was known for his extreme conservatism, after his death his widow, Joan Kroc (at that time the largest single shareholder in the company), donated millions of dollars for a research center to study world peace at Notre Dame University, to build a hospice in San Diego, California, to fund AIDS research, and to build a shelter for San Diego's homeless people. She also ran ads supporting a nuclear freeze. As owner of the San Diego Padres baseball team she helped a pitcher enter a drug rehabilitation center. However, when he was again found with drugs, she cut him from the team, though it cost her a million dollars to buy up his contract. She also banned alcoholic beverages from the clubhouse, a move that was hardly popular with the team. All these activities were made possible from the wealth that had been accumulated by her husband because of the success of the McDonald's Corporation.

On the negative side, some environmentalists charged McDonald's with using beef from cattle ranches in Latin America in the mid-1980s, thereby contributing to the destruction of the tropical rain forest and the increasing greenhouse effect. The company vociferously denied the allegation and threatened to sue one magazine, German-based *Natur,* for making false charges. In 1986 the Rainforest Information Centre in Australia reported it had received information that McD's used only U.S. beef in its American hamburgers but that the company did have franchises in Guatemala, El Salvador, Honduras, and Panama in which local beef was used as part of a program to support the local economy. The information suggested that Central America's rapidly growing population was probably responsible for more rain forest destruction than U.S. youngsters eating hamburgers.

In 1985 McD's initiated a new PR campaign, "Eating right—Feeling fit," aimed at elementary school children. The campaign included videotapes with famous athletes Bruce Jenner and Mary Lou Retton talking about fitness and good nutrition and a special edition of *McDonaldland Fun Time* magazine in which Retton and company clown Ronald McDonald gave fitness and nutrition advice. An official for the American Heart Association claimed that of the three largest hamburger makers McD's had done the least to provide lower-fat, lower-salt food items. A spokesman for McD's replied that the company was merely trying to provide consumers with information that would enable them to make more informed choices. In 1987 the attorney generals of California, New York, and Texas charged the company with deceptive advertisements that presented its food as nutritional. In a letter to the company, the attorney generals stated that four products listed in an ad (regular fries, regular cheeseburger, six-piece McNuggets, and vanilla milk shake) had not had their sodium content lowered over the previous year.

Though the authors of *The 100 Best* cited McD's for strong employee programs, they refused to include the company in their 1984 listing of the hundred best. The company scored well on the five criteria used in the study (pay, benefits, job security, chance to move up, ambience), but the authors argued that McD's is the largest employer of teenagers in America and profit is "squeezed out of the business by . . . low wages . . . and an assembly-line operation that leaves the employee with little or no free time to think." In 1987 Congress began hearings on raising the minimum wage from $3.35 to $4.65 per hour, the first such raise since 1981. Thirty-six business groups (including fast-food restaurant chains such as Kentucky Fried Chicken) formed the Minimum Wage Coalition to Save Jobs in order to combat union support for the change. In a surprising move, McD's announced through a spokeswoman: "We believe that minimum wage is a societal issue, best settled by Congress. We don't look at this as our issue." What McD's had done was to break ranks with the traditional, across-the-board fast-food industry resistance to raises in the minimum wage. However, a study of fast-food restaurants by the Philadelphia Unemployment Project in November 1989 found that workers in city outlets made an average of $3.82 per hour, compared with their suburban counterparts, who made $4.82 per hour. In addition, 77 percent of inner-city workers were minorities, while 67 percent of suburban workers were whites. In March 1990 the Campaign for Fair Wages, a coalition of church and labor leaders, initiated a boycott of Philadelphia's forty-five McDonald's outlets.

Just what is a socially concerned investor to do with the many pluses and minuses for McDonald's social features? Several responses are obviously possible. The authors of *The 100 Best* decided that the company did not deserve being on their list, but GOOD MONEY early included McD's on its thirty stock industrial average for socially responsible companies. GOOD MONEY decided that the company deserved to be the try-harder in the fast-food industry since McDonald's had a record of responding to a variety of social issues. As Boston-based radio talk-show host Gene Burns is fond of saying, "That's why they make chocolate and vanilla ice cream." Different people come to different conclusions about what is more or less important.

In precisely the same way, investors might disagree about the purely financial aspects of McD's. Indeed, some financial analysts argue that the days of explosive growth for fast-food companies are over, as the market has become saturated in both the United States and other parts of the world. Others, however, argue that managerially aggressive and innovative companies such as

McD's still have a lot of growth left in new products (McD's recently introduced several varieties of salad) and nontraditional locations (for example, a fast-food service inside a hospital or corporate headquarters). The fact that there are diverse financial opinions available to investors does not seem to befuddle them. Therefore, the fact that there are diverse social opinions available should not be all that confusing.

THE TRY-HARDERS DO BETTER

While making social judgments, never forget that the point of investing is to do well economically. The accumulating evidence is positive. The try-harders appear to do much better over time than those companies with irresponsible or nonresponsible social records. From 1980 to the end of 1989, McDonald's revenues rose more than 177 percent, while net profit climbed about 269 percent. Investors did even better. For the same period of time, the average annual stock price soared 566 percent and the declared dividends jumped 329 percent.

In order to test whether or not the same results could be found in other industries, GOOD MONEY Publications selected five companies that have been identified for being among the worst environmental polluters in recent years. The companies came from five different industries in which environmental pollution is a continuing problem. They included Dow Chemical, Occidental Petroleum, USX Corporation (steel), Waste Management (dropped from the GMIA several years ago because of serious environmental violations), and the Weyerhaeuser Company (forest products). These companies have been identified by Environmental Action as the filthy-five.

For comparison purposes, GOOD MONEY selected five companies in each of the industry areas with good to excellent environmental records and practices designed to deal with the inherent environmental problems in their industry. In the chemicals industry, H. B. Fuller (discussed in Chapter 1) was an obvious choice. In the forest products industry, Consolidated Papers (on

COMPANY	1980 to 1989 Change In		
	AVERAGE YEARLY STOCK PRICE	EARNINGS PER SHARE	DIVIDENDS DECLARED
Dow	+184%	+212%	+116%
Occidental	−3	−89	+30
USX	+62	−38	−13
Waste Management	+888	+578	+800
Weyerhaeuser	+30	+72	+38
Filthy-Five:	*+88%*	*−21%*	*+40%*
ARCO	+72%	+41%	+150%
Consolidated	+417	+213	+135
Fuller	+396	+52	+190
Safety-Kleen	+683	+423	+1,100
Worthington	+275	+198	+188
Try-Harders:	*+174%*	*+83%*	*+163%*

the GMIA) was selected for a good environmental record (tree planting, the use of wood wasters and hydroelectric power to generate electricity). In the petroleum industry, Atlantic Richfield (ARCO) had the consistently best-of-industry record during the 1970s and early 1980s (discussed in the next section of this chapter), as did Worthington Industries (on the GMIA), which was noted for state-of-the-art pollution controls in the steel industry. In the waste cleanup industry, Safety-Kleen (which sells a cleaning service to vehicular, general industry, and related markets) has a consistently outstanding record, unlike some other companies (such as Waste Management). GOOD MONEY called these five companies the try-harders.

As the accompanying table shows, the five try-harders far outperformed the filthy-five during the decade of the 1980s, as measured by change in earnings per share. Investors did even better in increases in the average yearly stock prices and dividends declared per share. Furthermore, there was almost a clean sweep for the socially better companies. For the thirty comparisons made for the ten companies, the only lower performances for try-harder companies was the increase in earnings per share for H. B. Fuller (compared with Dow Chemical) and in the increases in stock price and earnings for Safety-Kleen (compared with Waste Management). However, these differences were small and partially offset by greater increases in dividends paid to investors. What these comparisons demonstrate is that even a small portfolio of the best-of-industry companies can collectively outperform a portfolio of polluters—many of the latter consisting of the stocks of companies preferred by traditional profit-only investors.

MONITORING THE CORPORATE CONSCIENCE

Just as proft-only investors must monitor their investments for economic changes, social investors must monitor their investments for changes in corporate social philosophy and practices. The Atlantic Richfield Company provides an interesting example.

Through the 1970s and early 1980s ARCO's philosophy was to achieve a maximum profit within the context of responsible corporate behavior, and the company tried to live up to its creed. In their 1980 study of the social features of 317 large U.S. corporations, Milton Moskowitz, Michael Katz, and Robert Levering noted that ARCO was the only oil producer ever to oppose the oil depletion allowance (an economic windfall for petroleum companies) and the first to support the diversion of highway tax funds for mass transit. In a 1976 study the company was recognized as having the best overall record in controlling emissions in the petroleum industry. In 1982 the company did away with its credit cards and passed a savings of about three cents per gallon on to customers at the pump. Not only did business increase by about 50 percent, but ARCO struck a blow to the buy-now-pay-later plastic-money mentality of the current economy. In the same year the company committed $8 million to cap natural oil and gas seepages from California offshore drilling sites with permanent steel pyramids (other companies had used temporary canvas caps). ARCO also had a reputation for constructing pipelines so that they would not interfere with the migrating patterns of animals.

In 1983 ARCO's subsidiary ARCO Solar announced a project to build for Pacific Gas & Electric the world's largest photovoltaic plant, a sixteen-megawatt facility designed to produce twice as much electricity as that generated in 1982 by all similar systems throughout the world. By 1984 ARCO Solar had manufactured more photovoltaics than any other company in the world. In 1987 *CEP Research Report* and other sources praised ARCO for having sexual harassment programs at all levels of the company and for having a policy for family illness that provided six paid days per year in addition to the standard forms of sick leave. The same year the company gave more than $11 million in philanthropy, 31 percent to education-related activities—particularly for urban precollege programs designed for inner-city youth. More than $700,000 went to sixteen universities and colleges to recruit and train minority students pursuing engineering, science, and business careers. In Alaska the company had an ongoing program to recruit and train Native Americans from Alaska for jobs at Kuparuk and Prudhoe Bay. Also in 1987, minority businesses accounted for almost 5 percent of ARCO's total 1987 purchases, up from 3.1 percent in 1986.

More good news arrived in 1988, when ARCO Solar announced a major breakthrough in the efficiency of its solar panels from 8 to 11.2 percent. Scientists believe that when solar panels become 15 percent efficient, they will become cost-competitive with other energy sources, particularly oil and coal. The CEP's *Rating America's Corporate Conscience* gave ARCO its highest praise for philanthropy and support of social projects. From the 1970s to the early 1980s the company had been willing to call in independent critics from the corporate responsibility movement to assess these programs and had published lengthy, publicly available descriptions, including the critics' assessments. *The 100 Best* gave ARCO its top rating for benefits, superior ratings for pay and ambience, and average ratings for job security and the chances to move up. However, potential problems were brewing for ARCO's socially responsible corporate culture.

In the mid-1980s the company reorganized, started to sell off its nonpetroleum-related subsidiaries, and gone were two of the leading architects of the company's social culture—replaced by two men trained only in engineering. It didn't take long for problems to appear. In 1987 the district attorney of Los Angeles charged ARCO with dumping oil waste water and sludge from a refinery into a municipal water treatment plant. The company pleaded no contest to the charge and agreed to establish a $450,000 college scholarship fund in environmental studies at the University of California at Los Angeles. The district attorney commented to the *New York Times* that the innovative settlement would encourage research and training on the problem of waste disposal and could serve as a public example to corporations of their responsibility to local communities.

In 1989 the *New York Times* reported that Exxon and Shell Oil had sold off their past interests in solar energy and that ARCO was looking for a buyer for ARCO Solar. What made this news particularly distressing was that it could be another example of U.S. companies shooting themselves in the feet. Solar energy had shown all the signs of reviving, as illustrated by the recent breakthrough developed by ARCO Solar. Japanese and West German companies were increasing their commitments to the development of cost-effective solar energy. Too, ARCO's move to leave the solar business came at precisely the time when there was heightened public awareness of the need to seek alternatives to traditional fossil fuels. However, the biggest blow to ARCO's social reputation came when the company announced its intent to support legislation that would open offshore areas of California and the Arctic National Wildlife Refuge to exploration. The company argued that the potential exploration in the Arctic involved a very small area (less than 1 percent of the coastal plain) and could be carried out with minimal impact upon wildlife and the environment. Concerned environmentalists began lobbying Congress and contacting ARCO's Civic Action Program office in Los Angeles in opposition to the legislation.

Exxon's oil spill at Valdez, Alaska, galvanized the SRI movement and brought all petroleum companies under close scrutiny. In a 1989 semiannual report to shareholders in the Calvert Social Investment Fund, the fund's chair D. Wayne Silby indicated that a number of shareholders had questioned the fund's investment in ARCO since the company had allegedly committed numerous violations of Environmental Protection Act regulations in the environmentally sensitive North Slope of Alaska and had aggressively sought drilling rights off the California coast. Silby responded to the shareholders' concerns: "At the time the Fund originally considered investing in ARCO, the corporation had a better environmental record than other major oil companies and a stronger commitment to the environment. In addition, ARCO had a reputation for progressive policies in the areas of affirmative action, philanthropy, occupational safety and disclosure of information. We have advised ARCO of our shareholders' concerns and we plan to attend the May 1 [1989] ARCO Shareholders Meeting in Los Angeles. Be assured, ARCO will be a subject for discussion at our next Advisory Council meeting [for the Fund]."

In ARCO's 1989 *Summary of the Annual Meetings* report to shareholders, the question-and-answer section touched upon all the issues of concern to some investors. In response to a question from a representative of the Calvert Social Investment Fund, a company official said: "We are proud of our record in Alaska. We feel we have met all of the requirements of our permits there. As you know, there is some discussion about that and we'd be happy to have you visit the Prudhoe Bay oil field and have a chance to see it first hand. While you're here, I would like very much if you would take the opportunity to talk to Bill Wade, the president of ARCO Alaska, Inc." Another shareholder expressed support of the development of oil resources in the Arctic National Wildlife Refuge and asked what the status of that project was. An ARCO official thanked the shareholder for the continuing support, urged further letter writing, and said that the congressional bill was being delayed from coming to the floor (probably because of the Exxon oil spill in Valdez). The official said that ARCO still believed that domestic sources of oil must be developed for economic and national security reasons and that it could be done safely. In response to a question about the sale of ARCO Solar, an official said that ARCO thought it should concentrate upon its core hydrocarbon business. Furthermore, the company believed that the near-term possibilities for solar energy related primarily to consumer goods, something ARCO wasn't very good at developing or manufacturing, and that large-scale energy-related aspects of solar power probably wouldn't be possible until early in the next century.

What does this example illustrate? Yesterday's corporate hero can sometimes become tomorrow's corporate villain. All this means is that ethically and socially concerned investors need to be vigilant. They need to track the social performance of companies over time. This is no different from the vigilance required to monitor a company's economic performance over time. Anyone who makes an investment and then goes to sleep is flirting with disaster. Yesterday's profitable venture can also rapidly become tomorrow's economic loss.

LOOKING FOR CORPORATE SAINTS

As the examples of McDonald's and ARCO illustrate, there really is no such thing as sainthood in the corporate world. However, sometimes a company will take an exceptionally responsible action even if it defies traditionally presumed sound business practice. In such a case, the company may appear to be eligible for nomination to sainthood.

Merck & Company has long been recognized as one of America's best-managed corporations with good records in quality products, treatment of employees, and community responsibility. In 1987 Merck announced a policy unheard of in the history of the pharmaceutical industry. A drug (ivermectin), developed by the company in the 1970s for use against livestock parasites, had been found to be a safe and effective treatment for human river blindness (onchocerciasis). The problem was that this use classified ivermectin as an "orphan drug." In the pharmaceutical industry an orphan drug is one that has no market and, therefore, no profitability. The industry practice had been to discontinue work on orphan drugs since money had to be recouped from sales to pay for continuing research and development. Giving away orphan drugs free of charge was considered the height of fiscal irresponsibility.

What made ivermectin an orphan drug was the fact that the disease primarily afflicted humans in third world countries, where both people and governments were poor. In addition, because of the lack of roads and medical facilities in these countries, there was no way in which the drug could be gotten to patients and administered by competent medical personnel. However, the need was desperate. Blackflies breeding in fast-moving waters developed *Onchocerca* larvae. When a fly bit a human, it infected that person with the parasite. The larvae quickly grew into threadlike worms (from two inches long in the case of males to two feet long in the case of females) that lived under the skin for up to twelve years. The offspring of these worms (microfilariae) migrated through the skin, causing severe itching (some suicides had been reported as a result of extreme itching), destruction of the skin, lesions, blindness, and, in some cases, deaths.

After much soul-searching, Merck executives decided to give the drug away free so long as it was needed by those who could not afford to pay. The World Health Organization (WHO) agreed to coordinate international efforts to eradicate river blindness with drug distribution programs in third world countries. In 1989 the *New York Times Magazine* reported that Merck had also established an independent committee, led by Dr. William H. Foege (head of the Carter Center in Atlanta), to supply ivermectin (trade-named Mectizan) to agencies, governments, private groups, and anyone else who demonstrated the ability to give it to patients responsibly. WHO's program to eliminate river blindness in West Africa is designed to treat 250,000 people per year in eleven countries. No one knows for sure how much the giveaway will cost Merck, but the company has put a market value on the drug of $3 per dose for those who can afford to pay. WHO's experience indicated that one dose of from one to two pills per year can kill the microfilariae responsible for the symptoms of onchocerciasis and make it difficult for the parasitic worms to produce more offspring in the human body. WHO has estimated that from 18 to 40 million people are afflicted with the disease, and more than 300,000 have gone blind. If just half the number afflicted bought two pills per year, the revenue for Merck would be around $150 million—a significant amount of money for the company to give away.

Was Merck's decision to buck industry tradition in dealing with orphan drugs fiscally unsound? In 1988 GOOD MONEY's Vermont offices received a telephone call from a stockbroker handling the account of a socially concerned couple. They were interested in investing in a socially responsible drug company. GOOD MONEY sent the broker information about Johnson & Johnson and Merck. The couple purchased Merck stock, and the broker called back to say how pleased they were to find a company that had done something so exceptional. In addition, no one can estimate the enormous goodwill Merck has generated throughout the world or how this may translate into future sales. Certainly, Merck's decision has had no discernible impact on its bottom line. From 1980 to 1989 the company's total sales grew 140 percent as net profit jumped upward 260 percent. Investors were also handsomely rewarded as the average yearly stock price soared 471 percent and dividends climbed 332 percent.

Annually *Fortune* magazine conducts a "Corporate Reputations Survey" of several hundred large companies appearing on the *Fortune* 500 listing. The magazine asks several thousand business executives and financial advisers to rank the companies on a scale from zero (worst) to ten (best) within four financial and four social categories. The social categories include ability to attract / keep / develop talented people, community responsibility, environmental record, and quality of products and services. For four straight years, from 1987 to 1990, Merck & Company finished in first place in the magazine's survey, thereby demonstrating once again that doing well financially and doing good socially can go hand in hand.

5

SRI HOW TO

"OK," you say, "I'm hooked, and I believe I can really make money by investing in ethically and socially responsible ways. But where, and how, do I start?"

To understand where SRI fits into the spectrum of traditional Wall Street profit-only investing, the distinction between technicians and fundamentalists is helpful. Technical investors rely upon formulas, charts, and other numerical calculations to tell them whether or not it is time to buy or sell an investment. Fundamentalists focus upon less quantifiable factors, such as the quality of a company's management, the potential market demand for particular products and services, employee morale, productivity within the company, and the like. Socially responsible investors are primarily fundamentalists, though technical analyses can also be helpful to them.

FROM TECHNICAL INVESTING TO SRI

In several basic books for the average investor in the early 1980s, financial analysts recommended that twelve measures of a stock's

CATEGORY	MEASURE	HOW MEASURED
Current performance	Current yield	Current stock price/current dividend per share
	Dividend protection ratio	Last 12 months' earnings per share/dividend
	Current price/earnings (P/E) ratio versus past performance	Current stock price/current earnings per share compared with highest P/E ratio for past 10 years
	Current earnings/price ratio	Current 12 months' earnings per share/current stock price
	Book value ratio	Current stock price/current book value per share
Current risk	Asset to liability ratio	Current assets/current liabilities
	Asset to debt ratio	Book value per share/debt per share
Long-term risk	Earnings stability	Number of declines of 5% or more in last 10 years in earnings per share
	Earnings growth	Percentage increase in last 10 years in earnings per share
Possible upside reward	Estimated annual gain ratio	Estimated total profit (average high stock price for last 2 years less current price plus estimated dividends for this year)/current stock price
Possible downside risk	Potential downside risk	Possible loss (current stock price less low stock price for last 10 years)/current stock price
	Gain to loss ratio	Possible profit (high stock price for last 10 years less current stock price)/possible loss (current stock price less low stock price for last 10 years)

NOTE: Measures for what might be considered good are for the mid-1980s. However, since the opinions of financial advisers about what constitutes adequate yields, acceptable P/E ratios, and the like change over time, these standards must be adjusted to reflect current market conditions.

WHAT CAN BE CONSIDERED GOOD

5% or more

1.5 or more

Current P/E ratio is half (or less) highest P/E average for last 10 years

Over 15%

0.70 or less

2 or more
Over 1.0

2 or less

7% annually compounded

Around 20% or more

Under 20%

2 or more

and its company's performance in five categories (of risk, performance, and possible reward) could be used to ascertain whether
or not an investment was a good one. The advantage of these
measures was that the information could be obtained readily from
such sources as the *Value Line Investment Survey* (at the local
library) and the *Wall Street Journal,* and individual investors didn't
need a complex computer system to make the necessary calculations.

The measures described in the table on pages 92 and 93 are
useful when investors want to compare the strengths and weaknesses of two possible stock purchases. For example, an investor
considering the purchase of the stock of a petroleum company in
the early 1980s might have been attracted by the relatively low
stock price (around $24) and extremely high yield (over 10 per-
cent) for Occidental Petroleum (Oxy). However, an analysis of
the company's stock performance in comparison with the stock
of Atlantic Richfield (ARCO) would have sent up danger signals:

MEASURE	ARCO	OXY	REQUIRED
Yield	5.8%	10.3%	5% or more
Dividend protection ratio	2.6	NMF*	1.5 or more
Half 10-year P / E ratio	9.2	14.5	current P / E half or less 10-year high
Current P / E ratio	6.6	NMF*	
E / P ratio	15.3	NMF*	over 15%
Book value ratio	0.97	0.88	0.70 or less
Assets to liabilities ratio	1.13	1.09	2 or more
Assets to debt ratio	1.8	0.6	over 1.0
Earnings stability	1	4	2 or less
Earnings growth	+45.5%	−3.4%	7%
Est. annual gain ratio	30%	14%	20% or more
Potential downside risk	60%	70%	under 20%
Gain to loss ratio	1.4	0.9	2 or more

*NMF means "not meaningful." The measure is either too high or too low to have any real meaning
because the company is losing money, its stock price is too high relative to earnings, dividends are being
paid while earnings are very low, etc.

While ARCO passed muster on seven of the twelve measures,
Oxy scored well on only one measure: yield. Were these good
indicators of things to come? As we saw in the last chapter's comparisons of the filthy-five and the try-harders, ARCO had done

much better than Oxy. An investor purchasing Oxy stock at the end of 1983 would have received a total gain (capital gain or loss plus dividends) of 36.4 percent by the end of 1987, through roaring bull and bear markets alike. An investor purchasing ARCO's stock would have received a total gain of 99.4 percent for the same period of time.

Different financial analysts recommend using different technical measures. For example, some claim that the stock price per share to sales per share ratio (PSR) is a better measure than the P/E ratio. However, all these types of measure have one major disadvantage. They may tell an investor something about a company's current and immediate past performance, but they don't measure what is happening in the marketplace or economy as a whole. As a consequence, other technicians use what they believe to be more comprehensive technical market indicators. The best known is the composite index developed by Robert Nurock and dubbed by "Wall $treet Week" host Louis Rukeyser "the elves." Nurock's elves signal whether it is time to buy, sell, or do nothing by using ten indicators that are graded weekly as positive, negative, or neutral. If the balance of all ten is plus five, this signals "buy"; if minus five, it signals "sell." The following are several examples of Nurock's ten measures showing how they are designed to identify such things as monetary factors and investor psychology:

MEASURE	WHAT'S BEING MEASURED	HOW IT IS MEASURED
Monetary factors	The level and direction of interest rates	Lower interest rates could signal business expansion and a rise in stock prices, while higher interest rates could signal tighter money, which could discourage borrowing, and depress stock prices.
Market momentum	The rate of change (up or down) in the prices of stocks	If the DJIA goes up more points than the average for the last month, a downward correction in stock prices is signaled (and vice versa). Also, if the number of new stock

MEASURE	WHAT'S BEING MEASURED	HOW IT IS MEASURED
		price highs are fewer than the number of new highs in the prior 52 weeks, a new market low is signaled and an upward correction can be expected (and vice versa).
Speculative risk	The degree of risk that investors are willing to take	If the weekly volume of low-priced stocks bought or sold is greater than the weekly volume of DJIA stocks bought or sold, increased speculation is signaled—a negative indicator for the market as a whole (and vice versa).

According to Nurock, his Technical Index has been correct 81 percent of the time in predicting what the market will do twenty-six weeks ahead, and it has been correct 97 percent of the time for fifty-two weeks into the future. This claim indicates one of the problems with using only technical indicators for investment decisions. It is an essentially short-term strategy for those who are in and out of the market on a weekly or monthly basis. Too, technical analysis places great faith in numbers to measure such nonnumerical things as investor psychology, and analysis of such things as "market momentum" in purely numerical terms removes investment decisions from the real lives of human beings making investment decisions and running businesses. There is no such thing as a marketplace or corporation without human input, and this input must be measured in different ways.

As a result, fundamentalists and socially responsible investors argue that though numbers can be helpful, what is really important are such things as the quality of a corporation's management, the quality and productivity of its work force, the quality of its products and services, and the innovativeness and responsiveness of the company's personnel to changing market and social needs. Indeed, fundamentalists argue that these types of things, which often cannot be measured numerically, are better measures of the profitability of an investment over the long term than purely technical measures. An example of the use of both technical and fundamental measures is *Fortune* magazine's annual "Corporate Reputations Survey," referred to in the last chapter.

COMBINING FINANCIAL AND SOCIAL FACTORS

In January 1990 *Fortune* reported the results of its eighth annual survey for 1989. More than eight thousand senior executives, outside directors, and financial analysts were asked to rate the ten largest companies within their industry groups. The raters used eight attributes of reputation, four of which involved corporate characteristics reflecting social responsibility (not merely business ability): ability to attract, develop, and keep talented people; community and environmental responsibility; innovativeness; and quality of products or services. Four attributes measured financial reputation: financial soundness, quality of management; use of corporate assets; and value as a long-term investment. For each of the eight attributes of reputation, the raters were asked to use a score ranging from zero (poor) to ten (excellent). The survey involved 305 companies in thirty-two industry groups (in a few cases there were fewer than 10 companies in a particular group) that appear in the *Fortune* 500 and *Fortune* Service 500 directories. Industries with fewer than four major companies were excluded.

Merck & Company finished in first place with a score of 8.90 out of a possible 10, while Gibraltar Financial finished in last place with a score of 2.24. In addition to Merck, among the ten most admired companies were Minnesota Mining & Manufacturing (fifth place with a score of 8.21) and Wal-Mart Stores (tied for sixth place with a score of 8.16)—two companies also noted for social responsibility. Longtime social favorite Wang Laboratories finished next to last with a score of 3.08 primarily because the company had run into serious operating problems while founder An Wang's son was CEO.

Lest there be any doubt that social factors play a role even in the hardheaded business community, Exxon fell from first place (in 1989's survey) to sixth place in the petroleum industry category of ten companies with a score of 6.70. The reason appeared to be the company's totally inadequate response to the Valdez oil spill. Avon Products in the soaps / cosmetics industry category of eight companies finished last in everything except responsibility. Avon had been the target of animal rights activists until it agreed

GOOD MONEY COMPANY	OVERALL SCORE	FORTUNE'S INDUSTRY CATEGORY
Merck & Co.	8.90	Pharmaceuticals
Procter & Gamble	8.37	Soaps / cosmetics
Minnesota Mng. & Mfg.	8.21	Scientific / photo equipment
Wal-Mart	8.16	Retailing
Johnson & Johnson	7.91	Pharmaceuticals
Liz Claiborne	7.87	Apparel
Berkshire Hathaway	7.70	Publishing / printing
Corning Inc.	7.49	Building materials
Atlantic Richfield	7.47	Petroleum refining
Herman Miller	7.40	Furniture
Apple Computer	7.16	Computers / office equipment
MCI Communications	7.04	Diversified service
R. R. Donnelley & Sons	6.94	Publishing / printing
Dayton Hudson	6.84	Retailing
Digital Equipment	6.70	Computers / office equipment
Archer Daniels Midland	6.54	Food
Cummins Engine	6.47	Industrial / farm equipment
Norton Company	6.15	Building materials
Polaroid	6.02	Scientific / photo equipment
Hartmarx	5.98	Apparel
Pitney Bowes	5.74	Computers / office equipment
Avon Products	5.04	Soaps / cosmetics
Wang Laboratories	3.08	Computers / office equipment
Average for 23 companies	*6.92*	

NOTE: Some company scores were low because the industry group as a whole received low scores (for example, Building Materials and Computers / Office Equipment).

in 1989 to stop using animals for product testing. (See Chapter 7.)

The accompanying table summarizes how twenty-three socially responsible companies scored in *Fortune*'s survey. Note that, as a group, the socially responsible companies scored above the industry average.

RANK IN INDUSTRY	INDUSTRY'S AVR. SCORE	NO. OF COS. IN INDUSTRY
#1	7.08	10
#1	6.86	8
#1	6.27	10
#1	6.17	10
#2	7.08	10
#1	6.19	9
#1	6.87	10
#1	5.86	10
#3	6.69	10
#1	6.11	8
#3	5.63	10
#2	6.27	10
#5	6.87	10
#2	6.17	10
#4	5.63	10
#6	6.38	10
#7	6.61	10
#4	5.86	10
#6	6.27	10
#5	6.19	9
#6	5.63	10
#8	6.86	8
#10	5.63	10
#3½	*6.31*	*9.7*

These social favorites also did very well as a group compared with the total 305 companies in the survey:

RANGE OF SCORES	SRI COMPANIES		FORTUNE'S COMPANIES	
	NO.	%	NO.	%
7.0 to 9.0	12	52%	74	24%
5.0 to 6.9	10	44	211	69
2.0 to 4.9	1	4	20	7
Totals:	23	100%	305	100%

The social favorites also scored well according to the following measures:

SCORE MEASURE	23 SRI COMPANIES	305 FORTUNE COMPANIES
Mean	6.92	6.34
Median	7.04	6.08
Range	3.08 to 8.90	2.24 to 8.90
Mode	6.50 to 7.00[1]	6.50 to 7.00[2]

[1] Seven companies or 30 percent.
[2] Sixty-seven companies or 22 percent.

It should be noted that the socially responsible companies that finished with poorer scores in the survey primarily received low ratings for financial reputation attributes since they were experiencing operating problems at the time of the survey, not because they scored poorly in social attributes. What this survey indicates is that ethically and socially concerned investors are within the mainstream of traditional fundamentalism. As such, they do not reject financial factors but rather stress other types of indicators as also fundamentally important. Furthermore, the fundamental characteristics of a business can have a great deal to do with its economic success and rewards to the investor.

HOW TO AVOID GOING MAD

Rothchild and others may find SRI maddening, but the process is fairly simple. Here is a straightforward way for any socially concerned investor to begin:

Step 1.   Make a list of the financial objectives you want to achieve. These can include short- and long-term income, capital growth, or stability and preservation of capital. Since there is no such thing as an investment that can meet every financial goal, check the several that are most important.

Step 2.   Make a list of the social (or ethical) objectives you want to achieve. These can include any of the issues discussed in this book, or they may include special and personal values of the investor. Since there is no such thing as an investment that can meet every ethical and social goal, check the several that are most important.

Step 3.   Identify those investments that meet your primary financial and social goals and that, to the extent possible, maximize your other financial and social goals.

Don't forget that there are several approaches to SRI, as described in the first chapter. You can *avoid* offensive investments in companies that pollute the environment, use unfair labor practices, discriminate against women and minorities, make nuclear weapons, and the like. You can also *support* companies with good records for environmental protection, positive programs and practices for employees, affirmative action programs for women and minorities, quality and life-supportive products and services, and the like. In addition, you can *use your power as a shareholder*, in cooperation with other shareholders, to raise hell in order to change corporate practices.

As in the case of all investments, you should raise the question of what degree of financial risk you can afford to take. At the same time, the social risk of a potential investment can be assessed.

For any investment, there are four possible combinations of risk: both lower financial and social risk, both higher financial and social risk, higher financial but lower social risk, and lower financial but higher social risk. At the time this book was being completed, investments in the stocks of Volvo, Safety-Kleen, Digital Equipment, and Atlantic Richfield could be used to illustrate these combinations as follows:

Lower Financial and Social Risk: Volvo is a true SRI blue-chip company (and there are many more). The company has a long-standing record for producing quality products and for sound management. The company also has a long record for social responsibility.

Higher Financial and Social Risk: Though Safety-Kleen has a past record of good financial performance and good environmental practices, it is in an industry subject to high financial and social risks. By 1990 the waste cleanup industry had become a hot item on the stock market. As a result, speculation had run stock prices in the industry to heady highs. In addition, as the example of Waste Management's problems indicate, companies in this industry can rapidly find themselves among the polluters. Handling toxic wastes is a risky business.

Higher Financial but Lower Social Risk: Digital Equipment has a long-standing record for exceptional community commitment and treatment of employees. However, during the late 1980s Digital's earnings began to drop, as many companies in the computer industry found that more of their products were less popular in an over-extended industry (too many companies with too many different products). From 1988 to 1989 Digital's earnings per share dropped 15 percent, while the stock price dropped from a 1987 high of $199.50 to $82 by the end of 1989 (down 59 percent). The company began restructuring and developing new and more appealing products. Some financial analysts predicted a profit rebound sometime in 1991.

Higher Social but Lower Financial Risk: By any financial measure, Atlantic Richfield is a blue-chip company. After the company's new management took over, the company's net profits rose from a low of $615 million in 1986 to more than $1.5 billion in 1989 and the average annual stock price climbed 78 percent during the same period. However, as described in the last chapter, this financial success appeared to be at the expense of ARCO's longtime commitment to social responsibility. Many socially concerned investors believed that the company's past commitment to social responsibility was no longer present and that the social risk for this investment was now unacceptable.

There are five strategies available to investors for determining the degree of social risk that is acceptable for their investments: all or nothing, proportionate impact, best of industry, primary versus secondary involvement, and actual versus potential problems. These vary in degree of complexity, and each has special strengths and weaknesses. However, they are not mutually exclusive, and a number of the strategies can be used together in making an investment decision and for screening a portfolio. The table on page 104 provides examples for two social issues (South Africa and war work) of the kinds of questions socially concerned investors need to ask to implement these strategies.

Begin by determining which of your social screens you want to implement on an all or nothing basis. To what extent do you want your portfolio to be "completely clean" by avoiding investments in all companies doing business in South Africa or having defense contracts of any kind? This strategy is the most demanding, but it is not impossible to implement for some social issues. However, it may be difficult in other cases.

Since fewer U.S. companies are doing business with and in South Africa, there are many investment opportunities in companies that don't. Similarly, many companies do not have defense contracts of any kind. In contrast, because of the nature of modern industrial technology, there is practically no such thing as a business activity that does not alter or harm the natural environment to some degree. A rigid all or nothing strategy for environmental issues could shut out whole industries that characteristically have fairly high levels of environmental pollution—for example, chemicals, pharmaceuticals, and steelmaking. (Environmental investing is discussed in Chapter 7 in detail.) For this reason, many concerned investors turn to other strategies.

The strategy of proportionate impact can be implemented by asking what degree of involvement with a particular social issue

STRATEGY	SOUTH AFRICA	DEFENSE CONTRACTS
All or nothing	Should I avoid investments in all companies doing business in and with South Africa?	Should I avoid companies with any defense contracts whatsoever, regardless of service or product?
Proportionate impact	Should I avoid companies with 5% or more of their annual revenues from business in South Africa, or should I screen for type of service or product?	Should I avoid companies with 5% or more of their annual revenues from defense contracts, or should I screen for type of product or service?
Best of industry	Should I invest in companies doing business in South Africa but having good records for the hiring, training, and promotion of minorities and for opposition to apartheid?	Should I invest in companies involved in defense contracts but without records for fraud, cost mischarging, shoddy work, and other illegal and unethical activities characteristically associated with war work?
Primary versus secondary involvement	Should I invest in diversified and conglomerate companies that may have a subsidiary doing business in South Africa?	Should I invest in companies that do not have defense contracts but that provide services or products to (or obtain services and products from) companies that do have defense contracts?
Actual versus potential problems	Should I avoid investments in companies doing business in South Africa but having good records because the potential for involvement with apartheid and other problems is unavoidable?	Should I avoid investments in companies with defense contracts but with good records because the very nature of defense contract work is such that problems are unavoidable?

you are willing to tolerate in your investments. For South Africa and war work, this could be a very small portion of a company's total annual revenues or profits. For the environment, it could be a pollution record considerably below an industry's average.

However, concerned investors should be cautious about assigning arbitrary proportions when using this strategy. For a large corporation, only 5 percent in defense contract sales can allow many nuclear missiles to slip through a social screen. Proportionate impact judgments can better be made in qualitative terms. In terms of support for apartheid, there is a significant difference between Johnson & Johnson's selling of pharmaceutical products in South Africa and Ford Motor's sales of trucks to the South African military and police (which the company made at one time). There is also a socially significant difference between General Food's sales of food products to military PXs and General Motors' nuclear weapons work. Though only about 1 percent of AT&T's annual revenues come from the company's management of Sandia National Laboratories for the Department of Energy, the facility works on the triggers that detonate nuclear weapons.

The proportionate impact strategy can help identify the best of industry (discussed in Chapter 4). For example, a study in 1985 disclosed that of 317 companies doing business in South Africa, 175 had signed the Sullivan Principles, a set of guidelines for providing equal employment opportunities and for putting pressures on the South African government to eliminate apartheid, which were devised by GM board member the Reverend Leon H. Sullivan. About 25 percent of the signators to these principles had good records for trying to implement them in their South African operations.

One problem with this strategy, however, is that in some industries being the "best" may be offset by other factors. A congressional study in 1986 disclosed that eight of the top ten U.S. defense contractors had multiple allegations of fraud, kickbacks, false product claims, and other illegal and unethical violations. Only two, Hughes Aircraft (now owned by General Motors) and Litton Industries, had no allegations or pending investigations for these types of misdeeds. However, these two companies were still in the business of making dangerous weapons.

You must also decide whether or not you want your investments to be screened for a secondary, as well as primary involvement with a social issue. Some large, conglomerate parent companies (such as the Royal Dutch / Shell Group) may not be directly doing business in South Africa, but they may own smaller subsidiaries that do business there. In 1986 officials of defense contractor Raytheon Company announced that an agreement had been signed with the Digital Equipment Corporation to build militarized versions of Digital's civilian VAX computers. Digital was to provide information and design, and Raytheon was to make advanced computer chips for the converted computers. Conversion was required in order for the computers to hold up under shock, vibrations, extreme temperatures, and radiation on planes and ships and in tanks and trailers. When queried, a spokesperson for Digital denied that the company was involved in war work since the contracts were "secondary ones."

Finally, you must decide if you want to avoid investments with a potential exposure to social issues even if the investment's social record has been good. If widespread revolution comes to South Africa, companies with significant exposure in that country will not do well, regardless of their past records for opposing apartheid. Violent turmoil is not good for business. When peace began to break out in Eastern Europe in 1989, the stocks for most the U.S. aerospace companies began a steady slide downward. This slide barely reversed itself for only a few of the companies when the U.S. military buildup began in the Persian Gulf.

PRINCIPLES FOR SRI

As this chapter has indicated, investing responsibly is not impossible, nor does it have to result in an investor's agonizing about all kinds of ethical and moral issues. The principles that an investor can use to combine financial and social goals and values can be summarized as follows:

> *Principle 1.*　Start by determining your financial needs and goals. In other words, start where any investor does. Do you want security, high income, or the opportunity to make large capital gains? Since you won't be able to do all these things at once, identify the most important.
>
> *Principle 2.*　Identify your most important social concerns. Don't try to solve all the problems of the world at once. Make priority judgments about what you consider the most important social issues at this

time. Weigh the clear social positives against any potential social negatives in an investment decision.

Principle 3.   Keep your ethically absolute social screens to a minimum. There is no such thing as complete ethical purity in the social world. A long list of absolutes covering every imaginable sin will simply make prudent investing impossible. However, it is possible and relatively simple to screen for some types of absolutes.

Principle 4.   Decide what your investment can accept in terms of financial risk, and contrast this with potential social benefit. Would you be willing to increase some economic risk because the potential social benefit is so great? Would you be willing to sacrifice some economic return because the potential social return is so great?

Principle 5.   Decide what social risks are involved in your investment. Remember that there may be sound financial reasons for avoiding investments that are associated with socially undesirable factors.

Assessing both economic and social costs and benefits calls for a different type of thinking from traditional cost-benefit analysis in business. Traditional cost-benefit analysis deals only with dollars. Costs are seen as economic minuses and benefits as economic pluses. If it costs a million dollars to put in pollution control devices, this amount must be recaptured somewhere else so that profit is maintained. With the introduction of social costs and benefits, however, that equation changes dramatically. Pollution obviously entails social costs, but those social costs might also be associated with economic costs. Unhealthy employees are not productive, and communities don't want industries that pollute the environment. Therefore, spending money on pollution control can result in happier customers and consumers, increased sales, and higher profits. In other words, introducing ethical and social judgments into economic behavior not only does not create confusion or lessen the soundness of economic decisions but does make the likelihood of better economic decisions more probable.

Don't forget that having a social conscience can sometimes pay off in very unexpected ways. Recall how Smith College avoided a later stock loss when Firestone Tire's stock was sold because the company would not answer questions about its policy in South Africa. In a similar way, several chemical companies recently discovered that a social conscience was also good for business. Ciba-Geigy donated $50,000 to an environmental group to hire specialists to evaluate the company's plan to clean up contaminated sites. Was that $50,000 lost? Not really. The specialists noticed an important omission in the plans that neither the company nor federal regulars had spotted, and the company agreed to remedy the oversight. By so doing, Ciba-Geigy probably avoided future costly lawsuits or fines for environmental violations. Rohm & Haas spent $5 million analyzing the handling of dangerous chemicals. As a result of the analysis, the company modified its handling process. The modifications resulted in reduced inventories, which, in turn, resulted in lower inventory-related costs— costs that can be substantial for toxic chemicals.

Similarly, when the Massachusetts-based Stride Rite Corporation (on the GMIA) practically invented the idea of corporate day-care and educational services in 1971, the company discovered that it was not only good social policy but also good for business. In 1989 the company's CEO, Arnold Hiatt, testified before the U.S. Senate Labor and Human Resources Committee that his company did not start the Roxbury program for business reasons but rather because of concern about the failure of federal worker-training programs. The company wanted to intervene earlier in the child's development cycle as a good corporate citizen.

However, the company (the leading marketer of high-quality children's shoes) rapidly discovered that providing day-care services was good for business. Hiatt estimated that Stride Rite saves about $25,000 per employee, since the services reduce turnover and absenteeism and money does not have to be spent to train replacement employees. In addition, some of the first children at the company's Roxbury center now work for the company. Hiatt pointed out that the cost of providing good child care in Stride Rite's Cambridge and Roxbury facilities is about $7,000 per year. In contrast, the cost of maintaining a troubled adolescent in a group home is $50,000.

These day-care costs to the company have had no noticeable impact on the bottom line. From 1980 through 1989, Stride Rite's total sales increased 174 percent while net profit soared 633 percent. For investors, the average annual stock price climbed an eye-popping 1,177 percent over the same period.

6

YOU DON'T
HAVE TO BE A
MILLIONAIRE

Boston *Globe* business columnist Beatson Wallace has pointed out that there are many reasons why everyone should learn some rudimentary rules of finance and investment. A spouse may die; a relative may remember you in a will; bank accounts and IRAs, even though small, require some kind of monitoring. Nevertheless, many people believe that their chances of accumulating enough wealth to worry about is slim. Comedian Henny Youngman put it this way: "I've got all the money I'll ever need if I die by four o'clock." Unfortunately, this view obscures several important things.

Most people have an ownership interest in some sort of traditional market investment, even though they may not recognize it. In presentations before large audiences, Tim Smith of the Interfaith Center for Corporate Responsibility uses the following illustration. He begins by asking how many people in the audience do not own stocks or bonds, and about 80 to 90 percent of the people in the audience raise their hands. Next, he asks how many people work for a company that has some type of retirement or pension plan with investments in stocks and bonds, and at least half the people raise their hands. He then asks how many people have children in college or universities that have traditional investments or how many in the audience are members of churches or other organizations that have investments. Most of the people raise their hands. Finally, he asks how many people pay taxes to municipalities, states, and the federal government, all of which have investments. Everyone in the audience raises his or her hand.

In other words, almost everyone has some connection to traditional investments in one way or another. The important point is that these investments belong to the people, not the money managers. The people in a democracy have a right and obligation to say something about how that money is made and used. As Thomas Jefferson observed, "All authority belongs to the people."

Around October 19, 1988, the anniversary of the 1987 stock market crash, magazines, newspapers, and television featured experts and their opinions about what had happened and what could happen in the future. It became an unquestioned article of faith for almost all the experts that the individual investor—the little person—had left the marketplace for safer financial havens or had been driven out because he or she had lost everything. Like all articles of faith, this was really only a half-truth. To be sure, the crash drove out hundreds of individual investors who had made personal purchases of stocks and bonds. However, the "little people" were still very much in the marketplace in terms of pension, retirement, and other funds. Though these funds were managed by professional money managers, the money belonged to laborers, secretaries, college teachers, state employees, and the like. In addition, by early 1990 the small investor had begun coming back to the market by investing in mutual, money market, and other funds.

Ethical and social investing, therefore, is not something reserved only for wealthy individuals and big institutional investors. SRI is something in which every citizen, of whatever financial means, can participate. Ethical choices can be made during such simple activities as opening a small checking or savings account or putting $1,000 into a fund. A popular saying in the nineteenth century was that the U.S. railroads were built with the nickels and dimes of widows and orphans, who bought bonds to fund railway expansion. Similarly, modest investments of average citizens represent an enormous social and political resource.

SOCIALLY RESPONSIBLE BANKING

The idea of socially responsible banking is not an oxymoron. Increasing numbers of banks offer opportunities for small depositors that make sure their money is safe, is not used for questionable economic or social purposes, and goes toward positive economic and social development. You do not have to rely only upon your troubled neighborhood savings and loan or big local bank that redlines (refuses loans to) minority communities in favor of loans to faraway dictators.

Several years ago the Bank of California announced that it would no longer buy loans from other banks (a banking practice known as risk selling and buying) because it was extremely difficult to monitor loans and debt outside the state. First Virginia Banks (on the GMIA) has no foreign loans or oil patch exposure and concentrates upon consumer and mortgage loans within the state. From 1980 through 1989, a time when many of the country's largest banks were experiencing increasing economic problems, First Virginia's total assets increased 226 percent and its net profit climbed 338 percent. The bank's average annual stock price more than kept pace with an increase of 357 percent.

In a 1984 article for the GOOD MONEY newsletter, Steven Lydenberg reported that about two hundred banks and S&Ls were owned by African-Americans, women, Hispanics, Asians, and Native Americans and that more than one hundred community development credit unions emphasized redevelopment in both urban and rural areas. For example, the American Indian National Bank in Washington, D.C.—chartered in 1973—provides accessible capital for Native Americans throughout the United States. Of particular importance is a program to finance Native American-owned businesses. Another example is the Union Settlement

Credit Union, which from 1957 to 1984 had made loans of $12 million to East Harlem residents. During that period Union's default rate had been only 1 percent, far below the default rate for more "traditional" bank loan funds.

One of the best-known examples of a community-oriented bank is the South Shore Bank of Chicago. In the 1950s and 1960s the South Shore district changed from a predominantly white ethnic community to 95 percent African-American by 1973. Between 1969 and 1979 median family income fell from 10 percent above to 15 percent below the average for the city of Chicago as a whole. By 1980, 23 percent of South Shore families had incomes below the poverty level, more than 13 percent of the work force was unemployed, and more than 17 percent of all households were headed by women with children. In 1972 socially concerned banker Ronald Grzywinski stepped into this caldron and, with a group of concerned investors, purchased the struggling bank from a parent company that wanted out. This was the beginning of a very atypical banking story.

Complete rehabilitation and redevelopment of the district were necessary since during the years of white flight absentee landlords had allowed buildings to deteriorate and merchants had closed their shops and left. The new bank owner went into the community to ask for mortgage applications, loans for struggling merchants, and personal loans. The year before its purchase South Shore Bank made only two loans to local residents. Yet in 1976 the new management made sixty-five loans to more than half of all those who applied.

The fact that banks cannot initiate large-scale projects or invest equity capital is used as an excuse by many banks for not becoming involved in rehabilitation and redevelopment projects. However, South Shore Bank overcame this problem in 1978 by helping organize three separate companies under one holding company:

City Lands Corporation: a real estate development company to rehabilitate residential and commercial properties for rental or sale

The Neighborhood Fund: a fund to provide equity capital and loans to minority businesses

The Neighborhood Institute: a social development subsidiary to promote job training and placement and low-income cooperative housing development

Achieving financial solvency was not easy. Within two years
the once-sick bank was profitable and had increased deposits by
$7 million. In addition, the bank kept very unusual banking hours
to suit its working-class depositors and borrowers. Nevertheless,
except for loans to McDonald's franchises, the results were not
good. Many of the businesses failed, and the main street of the
South Shore, Seventy-first Street, still looked as bad as it had in
1972. Throughout the 1970s South Shore's profits were in the
bottom 25 percent for U.S. banks. It was at this point that a new
strategy was emphasized: rehabilitation of abandoned apartment
buildings that had become targets for vandalism, arson, and drug
dealing.

According to the ICCR Clearinghouse on Alternative Investments, from 1975 to 1985, the bank and its affiliates extended
about 4,500 development loans and rehabilitated more than 3,800
rental housing units. It also helped place more than eleven hundred
people in private-sector jobs and stimulated directly and indi-
rectly more than $90 million of investment in the South Shore
community. In a 1988 interview for *Ms.* magazine, South Shore
Bank's Senior Vice-President Joan Shapiro said that the bank had
enabled "a cadre of ma-and-pa rehabbers to restore over 4,500
units" of living space to the once-dying community.

The bank was assisted by offering development deposits at
competitive market rates and in amounts of $2,500 or more to
socially concerned investors, churches, and other groups interested in local community development. By the 1980s properties
in the South Shore district had regained their values without gen-
trification, and both public and private investment in the community was increasing. In 1988 Shapiro told *New Options*
newsletter that those people who had invested in the development deposits and who received market rate returns had been the
key to South Shore Bank's and the neighborhood's success. At
that time these deposits, which came from outside the immediate

neighborhood, made up 40 percent of all the bank's deposits and constituted a $59 million portfolio.

When the bank began lending on the neighborhood's decaying buildings, borrowers agreed to rehabilitate their properties and put money in escrow for maintenance. Thus, in a multiplier effect, each new loan reinforced previous loans. In addition, mortgage and rehabilitation lending created a group of entrepreneurs who, in turn, began to invest in the neighborhood's basic resource—its housing—thereby diminishing absentee ownership. In 1986 the bank began a program to help women enter business. Though it took about ten years for South Shore Bank to see the light at the end of the tunnel, its experience can be a model for ways in which local financial institutions, companies, and nonprofits can work together to encourage local community economic and social development.

A similar experience can be found in the case of Peoples National Bank of Commerce in Liberty City, Florida. Purchased by a socially concerned banker in 1983 with the help of Liberty City businesspeople and Miami Dolphins football team owner Joe Robbie, the bank had $12 million in deposits, no progressive products, and no prospects for growth. By 1984 the bank had doubled in size, with deposits of $25 million and more than 2,000 new accounts had been opened. New products and improved financial reporting methods had been adopted. Because there were few banks competing in the local area, deposits could be attracted at lower cost, and this helped keep loan rates down and still allowed for higher profits.

In 1987 a team of commercial bankers, neighborhood housing providers, small-business experts, attorneys, and others began developing a Bank for Socially Responsible Lending in New York City. The BSRL was planned to be a full service for-profit FDIC-insured commercial bank, concentrating upon creditworthy markets that have been traditionally excluded from loans by traditional commercial lenders. These markets included low-income and moderate-income neighborhood housing, small manufacturing and business services, and small financial institutions such as credit unions and community-based loan funds. By the fall of

1990 the bank had completed selling its initial stock offering of $6 million, purchased by 248 individuals and institutions (including American Express, Metropolitan Life, and Time Warner) and was ready to open its doors to business.

The idea of socially responsible and community-oriented banking took a major step forward in 1988, when Social Banking Programs, Inc., of Brattleboro, Vermont, signed a contract with the Vermont National Bank (the second-largest bank in the state, with more than $690 million in 1988 deposits) to help the bank begin a Socially Responsible Banking Fund. The significance of this new fund was that it represented the first time a big, traditional bank had accepted the same challenges typically left to the smaller, more experimental banks, such as South Shore, Community Capital, and Peoples. The fund was unique in a number of other ways. It provided the small investor with the opportunity to open business and personal IRA, savings, and checking accounts and to purchase certificates of deposit (minimum opening balance for all of $500) and to open money market accounts (minimum $1,000). Furthermore, the money would be managed in a socially responsible way in two senses. Deposits in the full range of products available (all at competitive market rates) in the Social Banking Fund would be used for loans for affordable housing, education, small-business development, agriculture, and environmental and conservation projects. In addition, the fund's investments were initially screened by GOOD MONEY Publications for investments (equities and bonds) that avoided companies receiving a significant portion of their revenues from defense contracts, from nuclear power generation, and from business operations in South Africa, or having a history of unfair labor practices.

CHALLENGING BANKING MYTHS

The reason traditional banks have been reluctant to become involved in community development is the persistence of the following beliefs:

Poor people are bad risks.

Making social judgments limits choices, and this, in turn, limits possible financial return.

Lending money to small businesses, people in need of low- or moderate-priced housing, or struggling farmers entails lowering interest rates below market rates, thereby making profitability impossible to sustain.

Because of these beliefs, redlining became commonplace. In 1977 the Community Reinvestment Act (CRA) became law in an attempt to stop redlining by government regulation. It required banks to help meet community credit needs and regulators (such as the Federal Reserve Board) to monitor compliance by banks. Some progress was made, but—old myths die hard—the act dealt essentially only with housing needs, and the CRA relied upon sometimes lax regulation.

By 1984, however, some large banks had responded. Over a five-year period Harris Trust (Chicago's third-largest bank) lent more than $35 million and found that only $5,000 (a home improvement loan) ended in default; in 1989 it hiked its commitment to $50 million in loans. By the end of 1988 Harris's loans to low- and moderate-income neighborhoods were 14 percent of its total loans in its primary market area. A 1989 report in the *Boston Globe* indicated that the Bank of New England had the best record for banks in that region. As William Ryan, executive vice-president for community banking, told the *Globe:* "If we don't [lend money to low- and moderate-income neighborhoods], we're going to have a tough time getting the community to deposit at our bank. The profit of the bank [is] involved."

Community leaders praised the Bank of New England for meeting the spirit, not just the letter, of the CRA law. For example, in 1988 the bank sent 800 surveys to community groups asking for a report on its performance in meeting community needs. The bank had spent more than $10,000 on a survey that asked, among other things, if there were enough automatic teller machines in neighborhoods. The Bank of New England was the first bank in Massachusetts to sign an agreement with the Massachusetts

Urban Reinvestment Advisory Group (MURAG), specifying the types of loans, neighborhoods, and nonprofit groups that should be recipients. By 1989 some two dozen other banks had signed similar agreements with MURAG.

Representatives of MURAG also praised the Bank of New England for its invitations to attend and participate in quarterly CRA meetings. The law requires only an annual CRA meeting and does not say anything about meeting with community groups. (The Vermont National Bank also met with community groups to obtain suggestions about its proposed social banking program.) In 1989 the Bank of New England designed a loan program that required less documentation and paper work, smaller down payments, and less demanding credit references, and the bank analyzed every loan in low- and moderate-income neighborhoods that was turned down in order to make sure that loan officers were doing fair and conscientious jobs with their assessments. The *Globe* reported that in Rhode Island community groups cited the Fleet National Bank and Citizens Bank for special praise. In 1988 Fleet began a low-interest, $1 million revolving housing fund and printed descriptions of the fund in English, Spanish, and Cambodian. Both banks work well with community groups.

As more banks recognize that socially responsible banking, in the form of neighborhood development loans, can be profitable for the bank, for depositors, and for neighborhood residents and businesses, there will be increasing opportunities for small depositors to participate. In addition, the CRA provides depositors, small or large, with the ammunition to ask their local bank precisely what their money is being used for.

It is particularly important for investors and depositors to ask questions about how a bank is using their money since as this book was going to press, many savings and loans and some traditional banks were in serious financial difficulty. For the S&Ls, the reasons appeared to be the practice of borrowing in the short term to lend in the long term, a risky practice when interest rates are fluctuating, and high-risk investments in such questionable ventures as expensive commercial real estate and fast-food businesses. For banks, out-of-state or foreign loans and loans to finance corporate mergers or to build expensive condominiums had begun to sour.

As this book has emphasized, the making of social judgments in the investment process must be combined with the making of sound financial judgments. Simply because a corporation has socially responsible practices does not guarantee financial success. At the same time there is no evidence that socially responsible practices ever caused a corporation to fail financially. Financial failure results from bad business decisions or unexpected changes in economic conditions—not from good social decisions. Because a corporation is being socially responsible in one area does not mean that it is being financially prudent in other areas.

As this book was being completed, the Vermont National Bank announced that in spite of the success of its Socially Responsible Banking Fund, it was having problems in its traditional banking operations, and the Bank of New England declared bankruptcy because of loan defaults—but not because of loans for low- and medium-priced housing or local community rehabilitation. A helpful measure of a bank's overall financial health is the portion of total dollar reserves available to cover nonperforming loans. A late-1989 report in the *Boston Globe* indicated that the average percentage of reserve coverage to total nonperforming loans at the top five commercial banks in New England was about 55 percent, *over 47 percent* lower than the average for the country's top twenty-two banks. This kind of information is publicly available and can be used to indicate when investors and depositors—socially responsible or otherwise—should be fiscally cautious.

Another opportunity for small investors and people of moderate means to participate in SRI can be found in the increasing number of socially screened funds. Several decades ago there were available to the public only a handful of funds that screened investments for social issues, in addition to offering financial opportunities for capital growth and / or income. By 1990 over thirty funds with different types of financial and social requirements were available for small investors.

SOCIALLY SCREENED FUNDS

The oldest publicly available fund to use some type of social screen was the Pioneer Fund, started in 1928. During the following years the sin screen was applied to Pioneer's investments, and in the 1980s South Africa was added. The first socially screened fund with an extensive social screen was Pax World. When it was started in 1970, the basic screen was to avoid defense contractors. Other negative and positive screens were quickly added. In 1972 the Dreyfus Corporation added the Dreyfus Third Century Fund to its family of funds. The Third Century Fund avoids investments in companies operating in South Africa and seeks out companies with good industry records for equal opportunity, safety, health, and environmental impact. As a result of complaints from the SRI community that its social screen was too weak, the fund's managers began strengthening the screen in 1990. The first action taken was to drop some large defense contractors from the portfolio.

In 1982 socially screened money funds received a major boost when the Calvert Group offered both a mutual (Calvert's Managed Growth Portfolio) and a money market fund with extensive social screens to the public. Calvert's Money Market Portfolio was the first money market fund to be socially screened. Calvert had been managing about a half dozen funds of different types, some of which received special recognition in the financial community for their exceptional performance. Wayne Silby and other early founders of the firm had long wanted to design ethically and socially screened funds to add to their existing family of funds.

By 1989 Calvert had added two more socially screened funds —a bond fund (the first such fund with a social screen) and an equity fund—to its family of twelve types of funds. All four socially screened portfolios are known as the Calvert Social Investment Fund, and all four avoid companies producing nuclear energy or its equipment, companies operating in South Africa or lending to its government or to South African corporations, and companies with a significant involvement in the manufacture of weapons systems. The four funds also seek our investments in companies with safe products and services, employee participation in defining and achieving company objectives and goals, good equal employment opportunity, good labor bargaining records, and a commitment to human goals. By March 1990 Calvert's Social Investment Fund of four portfolios had investments worth more than $434 million.

Shortly after the appearance of Calvert's mutual and money market funds, New Alternatives Fund and Working Assets Money Fund were made available to public investors. New Alternatives, the first environmental fund, avoids nuclear weapons makers, petroleum resource and atomic energy companies, and companies doing business in South Africa. Through investments it supports companies developing solar, geothermal, and other renewable and alternative energy sources, companies that employ energy conservation programs, and companies involved in the production and the recycling of natural gas. Working Assets avoids weapons makers, nuclear power, companies supporting repressive regimes (such as South Africa), and investments in Eurodollars. It supports companies with good equal opportunity, worker health and safety, employee bargaining, and environmental records and companies that make generous charitable contributions. Working Assets also seeks out investments that support higher education, family farming, and small businesses. It was the second money market fund to be socially screened.

By 1987 three additional funds that had very special types of social screens were available. The Amana Mutual Funds Trust invested in companies that met the needs of Muslims and satisfied Islamic religious requirements. To accomplish this, Amana avoided investments in companies involved with liquor, wine, casinos, gambling, or pornography and banks and loan associations not sharing profits or paying any form of interest (according to Islam, interest is considered usurious and is thus prohibited). The Ariel Growth Fund, designed by an African-American financial firm and managed by Calvert, avoided investments in companies with business in South Africa and companies that were primarily weapons makers or produced nuclear energy or its equipment. Ariel sought out smaller, lesser-known, or undervalued companies with long-term growth potentials. By 1988 socially concerned investors also could choose the Parnassus Fund, which advertised itself as a contrarian fund—that is, it sought investments in out-of-favor, innovative companies that provided quality products or services, treated their employees well, and were community-minded. The fund also avoided investments in companies with South African operations or with weapons contracts, companies generating electricity with nuclear power, and those involved with alcohol, tobacco, or gambling.

By 1990 some gold stock funds also did not invest in South African gold companies, either as an operating investment policy or because of a Western Hemisphere focus. These included Colonial Advanced Strategies Gold Trust, United Services New Prospector Fund, and Van Eck Gold / Resources Fund. Also, in 1989 and 1990 there appeared a number of new funds that advertised themselves as environmental funds. During the 1980s a number of socially screened funds were designed for large individual and institutional investors. These included the Catholic United Investment Trust; the Connecticut-based Common Fund; Miller, Anderson & Sherred in Pennsylvania; and USTrust of Boston. USTrust was one of the first banks to offer trust clients a socially screened account. From the end of 1980 through 1989 the bank's screened accounts rose 293.5 percent, compared with a 279.3 percent increase in the S&P 500.

READ THE FINE PRINT

Small investors interested in putting their money into a fund advertising itself as socially screened should read the prospectus carefully and check out what kinds of investments the fund is making. After they had purchased shares in the Ariel Growth Fund in 1989, several social investors discovered that among the fund's investments was Caesars World, one of the largest casino-hotel operators in the world. Caesars owned and operated three casino-hotels in Las Vegas and Tahoe, Nevada, and Atlantic City,

New Jersey, at the time. Some socially concerned investors avoid investments in gambling companies not only for moral reasons but also because they are concerned about possible connections to organized crime.

Socially concerned investors should be most cautious toward the proliferation of funds advertising themselves as having environmental screens. By mid-1990 there were ten funds that advertised themselves as being plays on the growing environmental movement, but some did not live up to muster. In early 1990 GOOD MONEY Publications analyzed the ten top holdings of the newest environmental funds and found the following investments:

FIDELITY SELECT'S ENVIRONMENTAL SERVICES PORTFOLIO	FREEDOM ENVIRONMENTAL FUND	SFT ENVIRONMENTAL AWARENESS FUND
Attwoods PLC	Calgon Carbon Corp.	Air & Water Technologies
Brand Companies	Chemical Waste Management	Calgon Carbon Corp.
Browning-Ferris Industries	Ebara Corp. (Japan)	Chambers Development
Chambers Development	Klein, Schanzlin & Becker (Germany)	Emcon Associates
Chemical Waste Management		Harding Associates
Laidlaw Inc. (Canada)	Laidlaw Inc. (Canada)	Laidlaw Inc. (Canada)
Waste Management	Norit NV (Netherlands)	Metcalf & Eddy Companies
Western Waste Industries	Safety-Kleen Corp.	Ogden Projects
Wheelabrator Technologies	Technocell AG (Germany)	Wellman, Inc.
Zurn Industries	Waste Management	Wheelabrator Technologies
	Zurn Industries	

Though these three funds had some investments in companies with good environmental records (such as Safety-Kleen), two of them had investments in one or more of the largest waste cleanup companies with very poor records: Browning-Ferris and Waste Management. In addition, both Brand Companies and Chemical Waste Management had very close financial and operating ties to Waste Management. Ogden and Wheelabrator burn garbage, a process of waste disposal that troubles many environmentalists. It is also extremely difficult to monitor the environmental records of foreign companies, even though SRI is growing rapidly in European countries and elsewhere in the world (see Chapter 8). Finally, a fund screened only for environmental factors does not look at other possible social negatives, such as defense work, bad treatment of employees, and lack of commitment to the local community. By mid-1990 one of the best environmental funds with the most extensive social screen was the oldest, New Alternatives. Two of the newer environmental funds also had good records for avoiding investments in companies with environmental problems as well as other social issues (avoiding the country's largest defense contractors and companies doing business in South Africa). They were Merrill Lynch's Eco-Logical Trust 1990 and Schield's Progressive Environmental Fund.

If an investor believes that she or he has been misled by a fund's advertising or prospectus, the investor can file a complaint

TYPE OF INVESTMENT	INDUSTRY / SOCIAL AREA
Certificates of deposit	Local investment
	Minority lending
Common stock	Alternative energy
	Computers
	Entertainment
	Environment / conservation
	Publishing / printing
	Retailing
	Transportation
Commercial paper	Education
	Environment
	Mortgage lending
Government agency bonds and notes	Education
	International development
	Mortgage lending
	Small business

*On the GMIA.

with the Securities and Exchange Commission and with the Social Investment Forum. That is exactly what one California investor did after she had asked a self-styled environmental fund for her money back (full initial investment with no deductions for expenses or capital losses) and was refused. As this book was going to press, her SEC appeal was still pending, and she had consulted a lawyer in case the appeal was denied. Progressive Asset Management, a full-service SRI firm, was instrumental in helping her collect information for her appeal.

The accompanying table provides examples of past investments made by some of the social funds with the most demanding, extensive, and reliable social screens. (The social funds may not currently have investments in the same instruments for a variety of financial and social reasons.)

INVESTMENT	SOCIAL FUND
South Shore Bank	Working Assets
American Indian Bank	Working Assets
Ametek, Inc.*	New Alternatives
ASK Computer	Parnassus
Walt Disney*	Pax World
Zurn Industries*	New Alternatives
Deluxe Corporation	Calvert
Ames Department Stores	Pax World
Southwest Airlines	Parnassus
Nebraska Higher Education	Calvert
Kern River Cogeneration	Calvert
	Working Assets
Pacific Funding Trust	Working Assets
Student Loan Marketing Association	Calvert
Agency for International Development	Calvert
International Bank for Reconstruction and Development	Pax World
Federal Home Loan Bank	Calvert
Small Business Administration	Working Assets

TRACKING THE PERFORMANCE OF THE SOCIAL FUNDS

Comparing the economic performance of socially screened funds with the performance of profit-only funds and the market as a whole is difficult and tricky for several reasons. A particular fund's financial performance is purely a function of the fund manager's investment skills—plus a little bit of luck. It has nothing to do with whether or not a social screen is used. In addition, all funds have different goals, which can range from a very conservative "preservation of capital" to a speculative "aggressive growth." Therefore, grouping funds together for comparison purposes is not easy. Consider an example that appeared in a 1988 *Ms.* magazine article about SRI.

The social funds were prominently featured in the *Ms.* report. The magazine asked Michael Lipper, president of Lipper Analytical Services, to provide performance comparisons for the social funds, and he supplied the information that is summarized in the accompanying table. On the basis of these figures, the magazine's report concluded that the performance of the social funds had been "nothing to write home about." Only two (Ariel and New Alternatives) of the eight (or 25 percent) had outperformed the averages for all funds of a similar type during the time periods studied. However, there are several things wrong with this com-

SOCIALLY SCREENED FUND	TIME PERIOD	PERFORMANCE
Ariel Growth	1987–88	+26.84%
Calvert Managed Growth	1983–88	+72.87
Dreyfus Third Century	1978–88	+295.81
New Alternative	1983–88	+66.19
Parnassus	1987–88	−2.05
Pax World	1978–88	+225.84
Pioneer Bond	1983–88	+63.39
Working Assets	1987–88	+6.16
Eight social funds:		+94.38%

Source: *Ms.* magazine and Lipper Analytical Services, Inc. (November 1988).

parison, and quite different conclusions are possible.

Including Dreyfus and Pioneer with the other social funds is questionable since those two funds have had the weakest social screens. In addition, classifying a fund is a judgment call. Lipper compares both Calvert's Managed Growth Portfolio and Pax World with "balanced funds," which are funds that typically invest in a balance of different types of investment instruments. Actually, over time, both these funds have been primarily mutual funds— that is, the major portions of both portfolios were invested in equities. Only at special times (such as before, during, and after the 1987 and 1989 stock market crashes) have these funds sought out substantial positions in other, more stable investments. Too, a careful reading of the prospectus for each fund will disclose that Calvert's Managed Growth Portfolio is designed to emphasize long-term income and capital stability, not necessarily extraordinary capital gains. Pax World seeks income and the preservation of capital. In other words, rather than use gross categories of funds, it would be fairer to compare funds that match on the following financial goals: aggressive growth, capital growth, capital stability, income, preservation of capital, and safety of capital.

Using these measures, the Lipper comparisons for Ariel Growth (an aggressive growth fund), New Alternatives (a specialized environmental and natural resources fund), Parnassus (a contrarian, therefore aggressive growth fund), and Working Assets (a money market fund) are the fairest and most reliable. However, Michael

FUNDS AVERAGE COMPARED WITH	PERFORMANCE
Small companies' growth	−4.90%
Balanced fund	+83.53
Growth	+335.43
Natural resources	+49.23
Growth	−6.26
Balanced	+288.96
Fixed income	+68.28
Money market	+6.48
Eight funds averages:	+102.59%

Lipper has made no secret about the fact that he does not like SRI and does not think it can work. What would have happened if he had submitted performance figures for only the four most reliable comparisons to *Ms.* magazine? The conclusion of the magazine would have been been remarkably different.

For the time periods analyzed, only one social fund (Working Assets) underperformed its industry average, and that by a very small margin. The remaining three outperformed their averages significantly. Overall, the four social funds had an average performance of +24.29% against an average performance for the four averages of +11.14%, a performance difference of better than two to one. What would have happened if Calvert's Managed Growth Portfolio and the Pax World Fund had been included, so that comparisons had been made for the six funds most broadly and rigorously screened for social factors? Three of the social funds outperformed their averages and three underperformed their averages for the periods studied. Together the six social funds had a collective gain of +69.98 percent, while the six averages had a collective gain of +69.51 percent. For those who believe that such a difference is too small to be important, it is best to remember that very small differences over time can compound into substantial profits.

In conclusion, investors considering funds should remember several things, whether or not the fund has a social screen. Funds should be used by the small investor for the long term, not for "quick and easy" short-term profits. Beware of funds that advertise or promise the latter. Funds should be used for the long-term preservation of capital to meet future needs, a conservative—not speculative—goal. In addition, any fund's economic performance over time has to do with the financial skills (and luck) of the fund's manager in making judgments about such factors as the direction of the economy, potentially profitable investments, investments to avoid because of potential problems, and overall investor psychology in the marketplace.

The evidence indicates that the managers of socially screened funds can meet these goals at least as well as, and sometimes much better than, the managers of traditional funds. Socially aware managers are more likely to spot and avoid investment excesses that can lead to long-term losses. They also are more likely to find investments that are profitable because of positive social features. Funds are not the way to instant riches. But if you invest in a socially screened fund, you'll likely do just as well as—maybe a bit better than—you'll do in investments in traditional funds.

7

AN IDEA WHOSE TIME HAS COME

By the 1990s more investors recognized the traditional Wall Street wisdom about what constitutes profitable investments was not only often socially unacceptable but also frequently financially dead wrong. Nowhere was this more evident than in the belief that investments in weapons makers were good bets during the years of a ballooning defense budget. From 1986 through 1989 the stocks of twelve of the country's leading defense contractors did very badly as a group compared with the DJIA and the GMIA. Only one outperformed the Dow or GOOD MONEY's average for the three-year period, and this was before the unexpected thaw in the cold war in early 1990.

Increasing the social awareness of many investors during the 1980s were a series of economic and environmental disasters or near disasters, particularly in the nuclear power industry. In 1983 the Washington Public Power Supply System, a consortium of utilities building nuclear power plants in the West, defaulted on more than $2 billion in bonds sold to the public. The default by WHOOPS (as the consortium became sarcastically known on Wall Street) was the largest municipal bond failure in U.S. history,

DEFENSE CONTRACTOR	Change in Year's Closing Stock Price			AVERAGE 3-YEAR CHANGE
	1986 TO 1987	1987 TO 1988	1988 TO 1989	
General Motors (H Stock)	+29%	+31%	+22%	+27%
Boeing	−28	+19	+47	+13
McDonnell Douglas	−17	+6	−19	−10
Martin Marietta	+9	+5	+10	+8
Raytheon	−1	0	+4	+1
E-Systems	−11	−2	+6	−2
Rockwell International	−16	−4	+9	−4
Loral	−18	−15	−8	−14
Lockheed	−31	−18	−6	−18
Grumman	−30	−19	−22	−24
General Dynamics	−28	−25	−12	−22
Northrop	−35	−28	−37	−33
12 weapons makers	−15%	−4%	−1%	−7%
DJIA	+2	+14	+27	+14
GMIA	+5	+18	+28	+17

since the first occurred in 1839. On March 28, 1979, at 4:00 A.M., the cooling system of Unit 2 of the Three Mile Island nuclear plant (owned by General Public Utilities) outside Harrisburg, Pennsylvania, broke down. Radioactive water flooded the plant, and panic swept through the Susquehanna Valley. More than a decade later the cleanup had cost more than $1 billion, and Unit 2 was scheduled to be permanently entombed in walls of concrete.

On April 25, 1986, the Russian nuclear plant at Chernobyl, near the large city of Kiev, caught fire and exploded. An anxious world watched as thousands of people had to be moved from their homes, radiation blew as far north as Finland, where it contaminated reindeer herds, and thousands of acres of Russian farmland were contaminated for generations. Later that year the Union of Concerned Scientists announced that thirty-nine U.S. nuclear plants, designed by General Electric, had the same potentially flawed construction system as the Chernobyl plant. The Nuclear Regulatory Commission hastily revised earlier safety predictions and estimated that there was a 45 percent chance of a severe core meltdown accident in the United States within the next twenty years.

What made the failures of the U.S. nuclear industry so troublesome was the fact that dependence upon traditional fossil fuels was beginning to be associated with serious environmental pollution. What alternatives does a concerned investor have?

WALKING THROUGH THE ENERGY INVESTMENT MINEFIELD

Each year the Nuclear Information and Resource Service in Washington, D.C., tracks the number of notices of violations issued to electric utilities by the Nuclear Regulatory Commission. This is a good source for investors to identify possible problems ahead for nuclear-connected utilities. For example, by November 30, 1987, a total of forty-six utilities had received 1,205 notices of various types of violations at one hundred nuclear plants for that year. This was an average of slightly over 26 violation notices per utility. Twelve utilities received higher-than-average 1987 violation notices (number of notices received for the year in parentheses):

Southern Company (105)	Middle South Utilities (56)
Commonwealth Edison (95)	Carolina Power & Light (43)
Duke Power (75)	Detroit Edison (31)
FPL Group (74)	Philadelphia Electric (32)
Dominion Resources (63)	Centerior Energy (29)
Tennessee Valley Authority (60)	Illinois Power (29)

Some nuclear utilities—sadly, a very few—do have good and responsible records with nuclear power. One such is the New England Electric System (NES) which in 1989 generated 44 percent of its electricity needs with coal, 28 percent with oil, 13 percent with hydro and alternative sources, and 15 percent with nuclear power. The alternative sources included trash-to-energy technologies. Around the time of the oil embargo in the 1970s, NES had a 78 percent dependency on oil and the company's customer favorability rating had fallen below 40 percent, as measured by outside polls. However, by 1984 NES had embarked on an aggressive energy diversification and alternative energy program, and the favorability rating was more than 70 percent.

This success was largely the result of the efforts of retiring Chairman and CEO Guy Nichols, who was the first executive of a utility with a 10 percent share in the troubled Seabrook nuclear power project in New Hampshire to recommend publicly that one of the nuclear units be canceled. Also significant were the alternative energy views of Vice-Chairman Joan T. Bok, who had been a philosophy major at Radcliffe College and was a graduate of Harvard Law School. The company's executives had long been known for willingness to reach out to conservationists, consumer advocates, and watchdog groups of all kinds. These unusual qualities for managers of a nuclear utility obviously paid off in economic performance. From 1980 to 1989 NES's average yearly stock price climbed 151 percent, earnings per share increased 26 percent, and dividends declared jumped 70 percent.

The most obvious way for concerned investors to avoid the pitfalls of nuclear power is to seek out investments in companies developing and using alternative and renewable energy. Geothermal energy is a case in point.

In the 1800s a northern California hunter looking for grizzly bears stumbled into a valley filled with rattlesnakes and hissing steam vents. The smell of sulfur reminded him of hell. For years the region was a natural curiosity, and it later became a health spa visited by such famous people as Franklin D. Roosevelt. The Geysers fell into disuse during World War II, and the buildings of the spa deteriorated. After the war attempts were made to tap the geothermal steam to generate electricity, but excessive corrosion was so bad that the process was uneconomical. In the 1960s the Magma Power Company joined with Union Oil and Dow Chemical and eventually solved the corrosion problem. By the early 1980s Pacific Gas and Electric was obtaining more than 10 percent of its energy needs from The Geysers plant. Yet there was also an environmental problem. Hundreds of small quakes are experienced each day at The Geysers, as underground water is tapped. As a result, the plant developed a system to recycle used water back into the underground crevices.

Magma Power's performance for investors has been spectacular. In 1966 investors could have purchased Magma stock for around $1 per share. At that time the company's earnings showed a deficit of three cents per share, and the book value of the stock was around five cents per share. By 1981 Magma's earnings were $1.52 per share, the book value was $6.31 (up 12,520 percent), and a share of stock reached a high of $53.50 (up a whopping 5,250 percent). It should be noted, however, that investments such as Magma are highly speculative. The company pays no dividends. In 1982 the Natomas Company bought Magma Power for $45 per share and acquired the successful Geysers project. All other assets were transferred to a new company, and ten million shares of stock were made available at $3 each to shareholders owning stock on the date of transaction and in proportion to the shareholders' prior holdings.

The "new" Magma Power Company began developing other geothermal projects in California, and discussions were held with Mitsui of Japan to assist in the development of that country's substantial geothermal energy resources. In 1986 Magma owned 49,000 acres of land for geothermal exploration in California and Nevada and operated a ten-megawatt geothermal plant in Mammoth, California. After the merger with Natomas and the spin-off of the new company in 1982, earnings per share showed a deficit of thirty-four cents. However, by the end of 1989, earnings per share had grown to $1.01. Once again, investors were rewarded handsomely as the stock price grew from the initial offering price of $3 to around $35 in early 1990 (up 3,500 percent).

Generating geothermal power is environmentally sound insofar as it releases only negligible amounts of carbon dioxide (which contributes to the greenhouse effect) and no nitrogen or sulfur oxides (which contribute to acid rain). However, it is not without some potential social and environmental costs, as Hawaiian Electric

Industries (HEI) has found on the Big Island of Hawaii. HEI has long been trying to develop alternative energy sources for the state of Hawaii, including biomass, geothermal, hydro, wind, and ocean thermal energy conversion—in order to lessen the utility's 94 percent dependence upon imported oil. In 1982 the company opened its first operating geothermal well in Puna, Hawaii, and a contract was signed with the True Geothermal Energy Company of Wyoming to develop additional geothermal energy capacity on the island. Plans were made to lay an undersea cable from Hawaii to the islands of Maui and Oahu to supply these islands with additional electricity.

Initial opposition came from Native Hawaiians, who argued that such development was a violation of their religion, since they worshiped the goddess Pele, who lives in Kilauea volcano and creates the land, flowers, shrubs, and other vegetation growing on the island. The Pele Defense Fund was formed, and a First Amendment suit was filed in court. The Native Hawaiians lost the suit, and the U.S. Supreme Court turned down a request to hear an appeal.

Originally the state of Hawaii was going to permit drilling only at elevations on the slopes of the volcano above the lowland Wao Kele O Puna rain forest and on private land that had already been forested. Then, in 1983, Kilauea erupted, spitting out lava as deep as 300 feet over roads and the private land. In 1985 negotiations kept the project alive when the state traded the 25,000 acres of lava-covered private land for 27,000 acres of other land, including parts of the Puna rain forest, to Campbell Estates. The swap was challenged in court by critics who claimed that the new land was supposed to be used as a trust for Native Hawaiians in return for the land that had been partially logged and was covered by lava. In addition, geothermal drilling could release brine and hydrogen sulfide gases, which are extremely destructive to a fragile rain forest.

Some socially concerned investors questioned HEI's motives, but the real villain in this case appears to be the state government and Hawaii's insatiable appetite for tourism and more hotels, nightclubs, and restaurants with air conditioning, particularly on

Oahu. Not surprisingly, the state's leading businesspeople and politicians supported the geothermal development, but HEI appeared to be caught in the middle as a utility that was trying to meet its obligation to provide more electricity without having to depend upon imported oil.

Investments in utilities are generally known for security of capital and good dividend returns, not for capital gains. However, during the 1980s investors in HEI's stock did very well. From the end of 1980 through 1989 HEI's earnings per share rose 62 percent, dividends declared per year increased 66 percent, while the average annual stock price jumped 224 percent. Part of the company's success was obviously attributable to its increasing involvement with alternative energy sources.

ENVIRONMENTALISM AND SRI

In addition to energy, environmental issues appeared to be the most popular public concerns that would fuel SRI in the 1990s. When SRI first began, such bastions of conservative capitalism as *Fortune* magazine denounced it as do-good nonsense, corporation hating and insignificant in the long run. However, in 1990 the magazine carried a major feature story, "Environmentalism: The New Crusade." It pointed out that "some smart companies" were beginning to respond to environmental concerns in important ways, and it even carried a box that featured Franklin Research and Development's ranking for good and bad environmental companies in seven different industries (see opposite).

As Earth Day 1990 approached, companies scrambled to participate. The Shaklee Corporation paid $50,000 to become the first official sponsor for that year. Apple Computer and Hewlett-Packard donated equipment. Other companies announced major environmental programs. Du Pont planned to suspend voluntarily all production of CFCs by the year 2000 or sooner, though this was a $750-million-a-year business for the company, which was developing alternatives to replace CFCs in cleaning, refrigeration, and other uses at a possible cost of $1 billion. McDonald's

Some of the companies cited in *Fortune* and ranked by Franklin R&D for their environmental record:*

INDUSTRY	GOOD COMPANIES	THE POLLUTERS
Chemicals	H. B. Fuller	W. R. Grace
Computers	Apple Computer	IBM
Gas	Cons. Nat. Gas	Panhandle E.
Oil	Amoco	Exxon
Photo	Polaroid	Eastman Kodak
Steel	Nucor	Bethlehem
Utilities	Louisville G&E (now LG&E Energy)	Southern Co.

*Franklin uses a scale from 5 (worst) to 1 (best). For the good companies above, the scores ranged from 1.5 (Apple and Fuller) to 2.5 (Cons. Nat. Gas and Polaroid). The polluters ranged from 4 (Bethlehem, Eastman, and Panhandle) to 5 (Exxon and Grace).

made its drinking straws 20 percent lighter, thereby eliminating one million pounds of waste per year. All of the company's napkins in U.S. outlets, carryout drink trays, and paper at the company's headquarters were being made from recycled paper. Pacific Gas & Electric spent $10 million in cooperation with the Natural Resources Defense Council and others on a study of ways to improve the efficient use of electricity. The study used a computer model developed by the Environmental Defense Fund.

Wall Street analysts began touting the stocks of companies that would benefit from the environmental movement. These include:

Air & Water Technologies: provided services and technologies to control air pollution and to protect water resources.

Allwaste: was involved in asbestos abatement, cleaning the inside of tanker trailers, and the vacuuming of industrial wastes.

Calgon Carbon Corporation: produced and marketed activator carbons and provided related services and systems. These products were used to control air and water pollutants.

Church & Dwight: best known for its leading product, Arm & Hammer baking soda, was involved in a joint venture to develop a process for reducing sulfur dioxide and nitrogen oxide emissions by spraying sodium bicarbonate into industrial smokestacks.

IMCO Recycling: recycled aluminum beverage cans, dross, and scrap. Was the largest independent recycler of cans and the country's only publicly owned company providing this service.

Wellman Inc.: recycled plastics and fibers from reclaimed soda bottles, film, and waste and turned them into polyester and nylon fibers for carpets, pillow stuffings, automobile trunk linings, and tennis ball fuzz.

By mid-1989 some studies were beginning to demonstrate a solid connection between environmental protection and profitability. For example, traditional analysis had assumed that a rain forest needed to be cleared to maximize economic return and enhance development. However, *Nature* magazine reported the findings of a study of a section of Amazonian forest near Iquitos, Peru, which concluded that a live rain forest may be worth more than a dead one. The analysis argued that 1 hectare (2,471 acres) produces $400 in fruit and $22 in rubber annually. Since these types of products grow every year, the real value of the forest far exceeded one year's profit. Therefore, the total worth was estimated by the researchers as "net present value," which amounted to $6,330 per hectare, not including the value of medicinal plants and other products. (Plant life has been the source of penicillin, digitalis, resins, and insecticides.) In contrast, cutting 1 hectare of rain forest timber earns a net revenue of $1,000, and this is a one-time profit. For other uses, the researchers estimated the following net present values: cleared forest, $3,184; pastureland, less than $2,960; and tree plantation, only $490.

RECOGNIZING CORPORATE FLIMFLAM

As the example of Magma Power and the critique of the new environmental funds in the last chapter indicate, there are also many minefields for socially concerned investors interested in environmentally positive investments. So anxious were many companies to participate in Earth Day 1990 that some did such meaningless things as wrap their products in green packaging;

Environmental Action called those companies "camouflaged polluters." Some companies used advertising that ranged from not completely honest to downright deceptive (called the "Oat Bran Marketeers" by Environmental Action). Others touted their environmental awareness apparently in an attempt to cover up other sins (called "Dr. Jekyll and Mr. Hyde").

Alberto-Culver's Alberto VO5 hair spray was marketed as "ozone friendly" because it contained no CFC propellant. However, hair sprays can contain other ingredients, such as propane, that are not good for the environment. Amway claimed that its spray products had been free from CFCs for more than a decade. The catch was that the U.S. government banned CFCs from aerosols in 1978. The Mobil Chemical Company, a subsidiary of Mobil Corporation, marketed Hefty trash bags as degradable. The problem was that they would break down in sunlight in your backyard but not when buried in landfill. After complaints from environmentalists, Mobil agreed to drop the word *degradable* from its garbage bags.

During the Earth Day 1990 celebrations Champion International sponsored canoe and kayak races on four scenic rivers. None of those rivers was Pigeon River in North Carolina, into which the company's pulp mill legally dumps forty-two million gallons of brownish chemical-laced waste each day. Union Carbide promoted its recyclable plastic containers used for such products as Tab cola, Tide detergent, and Minute Maid juice. However, the company didn't talk much about its fatal 1985 gas leak in Bhopal, India, which killed and maimed thousands of people and animals, and the near repeat in West Virginia shortly after the Indian disaster. Nor did the company talk about how its executives stonewalled and obfuscated and did everything possible to block lawsuits by and compensation for those who suffered in India.

In ads that saturated Southern California's radios, television, print media, and bus panels, Atlantic Richfield touted its development of a new lower-emission unleaded gasoline in late 1989. However, as the *Los Angeles Times* reported, a funny thing happened on the way to the gasoline pump: Most people who saw and heard the ads couldn't buy the smog-reducing gas. ARCO was marketing the new gas only to owners of older cars and trucks, those without catalytic converters, and these accounted for only one out of every five gallons of gas bought in the Southern California market in 1989. Too, ARCO put the gas in pumps with large nozzles that don't fit newer cars.

The catch is something the company's ads forgot to mention. The new gas (a mixture of methanol and regular gasoline) can be used in newer cars and will lead to less air-polluting emissions. ARCO denied that the company was more interested in image than substance and claimed it simply could not make enough new gas to go around. That was certainly not the story that was first released by the company, government regulators, and other supporters of the new gas. Several months earlier ARCO had announced that the switchover was relatively simple and inexpensive (two cents per gallon, which would be absorbed by the company) and that the company would share its formula with other petroleum manufacturers to help reduce Southern California's major air pollution problem.

In fairness, it should be observed that a good deal of environmental pollution lies at the opening of the consumer's wallet, not just at the door of the corporation. In 1989 the *Wall Street Journal* reported that when Wendy's International and McDonald's considered a replacement of their foam plates and cups with paper ones, customers balked. Paper plates stain and paper cups leak. When Procter & Gamble offered Downy fabric softener in concentrated form, which requires less packaging, sales were poor because the concentrate had to be mixed with water. Eastman Kodak tested the idea of eliminating its yellow film boxes. The company found that professional photographers buying the film by the case didn't care, but small purchasers thought they were getting something of less value. When H. J. Heinz looked for alternatives to its plastic squeeze bottles for ketchup, which account for about a third of all ketchup sold in the United States, the company was worried because the kids wouldn't find it fun not to be able to squeeze glass. As a result, Heinz announced in 1990 that it was developing a packaging product called ENVIROPET that could be recycled by such companies as Wellman. This new plastic bottle was to be introduced in 1991.

Sometimes what at first blush looks like a good environmental idea can turn out to be not such a good idea after all. In 1985 the CMS Energy Corporation (then Consumer's Power Company) in Michigan had abandoned its Midland nuclear plant after a series of management disasters, which included building the multibillion-dollar plant on shifting sand. The utility was near bankruptcy when the MIT-trained nuclear engineer William T. McCormick, Jr., joined it. He used his skills as a former regulator and lobbyist to persuade others he could raise the Midland phoenix from the ashes by converting the facility to a cogeneration gas plant.

Though Detroit's Big Three automakers argued that the conversion would hike their electricity rates significantly, McCormick wooed Dow Chemical, an initial adversary, to support the project, and he enlisted the aid of CEOs of twenty-five big Michigan companies (including Federal-Mogul and Upjohn), many of whom played golf together. McCormick then sold equity shares in the new project. Next, he convinced regulators to classify $1.5 billion spent on the failed nuclear plant by CMS as "reusable assets" for the new venture. A General Motors executive unsuccessfully testified that this was paper work nonsense and that the real value of usable assets was closer to $300,000. The rest of the cost was the result of CMS mismanagement and should be borne by the company, not by ratepayers and the general public. Indeed, some observers believed that it would be far less costly to all concerned to build a new cogeneration gas plant from scratch.

In 1985 the Michigan Public Service Commission (MPSC) granted CMS a 5 percent rate hike amounting to $79 million annually as "financial stabilization" revenues to help rescue the company from financial collapse. When the new cogeneration facility went on-line in March 1990, CMS stopped collecting this additional amount since a $1.9 billion debt reduction requirement set in 1985 had been met. The MPSC welcomed cessation of the financial stabilization revenues but ordered CMS to post a

$450 million bond to cover potential refunds of excess revenues and to prove that the company had been in compliance with the 1985 order. Meanwhile, McCormick was stumping the country—with an eye on some twenty abandoned nuclear plants—trying to sell his company's expertise in converting nuclear sow's ears into cogeneration silk purses. This consulting role would not only bring in a lot of unregulated profit for CMS but also show others how they could build a power plant that could escape regulation.

ANIMAL RIGHTS AND SRI

Closely allied to environmentalism is the animal rights movement, which is beginning to have an impact on business and investing. The movement's goal is to stop gratuitous human exploitation of animals and demonstrate the human connection to and dependence upon all other life-forms. The entire ecosystem consists of special natural balances. Not only does the destruction of life disrupt the natural food chain, but it also eliminates forever possible benefits for human beings. Lower-order life-forms, such as snails and clams, are in danger of extinction from environmental pollution as a result of industrial wastes and dredging. Yet these forms of life can produce antibiotics, tranquilizers, antispasmodics, and antiseptic chemicals in their systems.

Of particular concern to animal rights advocates is the use of animals for testing products. This use persists for two main reasons. First, it is big business. Bausch & Lomb, for example, owns and operates the Charles River Laboratories, a company with worldwide facilities that breeds animals for sales to research facilities. Second, there is a widespread belief that there is simply no other way of guaranteeing human health and safety. However, as a result of consumer and shareholder action by animal rights groups, many companies are now exploring new laboratory techniques that use fewer animals, lower-order animals, or no animals at all for the testing of products. There are also some compelling scientific reasons for exploring these alternatives. If aspirin and penicillin had been tested in animals, they might not now be used by humans. Aspirin kills cats (often used in testing), and penicillin kills guinea pigs (very often used in testing). In addition, when thalidomide was tested on mice and monkeys, it was pronounced safe. We now know that human use of thalidomide results in children born without arms and legs.

Procter & Gamble used 174 dogs, 392 hamsters, 1,486 rabbits, 4,740 pigs, and an estimated 45,000 rodents (companies are not required to disclose the number of rodents used) in the year ending on September 30, 1985. While these numbers certainly are high, the company's reasons appeared to be compelling. It has to anticipate not only the safety involved with the intended use of a product but also its possible misuse. P&G estimates that about two thousand times a month someone, often a young child, swallows one of its cleaning products. Nevertheless, P&G states that it hasn't increased its use of animals in product safety testing over the past five years, in spite of an expansion in product lines. This lessened dependence upon animal testing has resulted from a change in what is known as the LD50 Test (lethal dose 50 percent test). This test for toxicity involves the painful force feeding of the test substance to large numbers of animals (usually 40 to 100 rodents and sometimes a few dogs and primates) until half of them die. The animals that survive are then killed and dissected, and a statistical determination is made about how toxic the substance was. What P&G has done is to use 1 rat at a time and gradually move the dose up or down until the lethal range is found. Fewer than 10 rats are usually needed now to complete a test.

Friends of Animals, an animal rights advocacy group, has pointed out that there are many viable alternatives to the use of any animals for much product testing. These include dummies in automobile crash tests, computer and mathematical models for toxicity testing, and the use of human tissue grown in the laboratory. In 1981 the Center for Alternatives to Animal Testing was founded at the Johns Hopkins University School of Hygiene and Public Health with start-up funds from a grant by the Cosmetic, Toiletry and Fragrance Association. Other corporate sponsors have included Abbott Laboratories, Amoco, Bristol-Myers, and Exxon. Unfortunately corporations and researchers have often been less enthusiastic and generous in their support of the search for alternatives. For example, by the mid-1980s the Cosmetic, Toiletry and Fragrance Association had donated about $2.5 million. However, 1985 sales for the six largest companies in this industry were $8.7 billion. The donation, then, was a miserly three one-hundredths of 1 percent of total sales. Mammoth Exxon had donated $50,000—an almost invisible portion of $86.7 billion in 1985 sales.

As this book was being completed, a major victory for the animal rights movement occurred. A representative for Avon Products, the world's largest maker of cosmetics and toiletries with annual sales of more than $3 billion, announced that it would stop using animals for product testing. This policy included the use of mice, rats, and guinea pigs. The company had been persuaded that it could effectively substitute tissue cultures, computer programs, and perhaps even plants. Shortly thereafter Revlon and Fabergé (which was being acquired by Unilever) announced that they had abandoned animal testing. Amway and Mary Kay Cosmetics declared a moratorium on animal tests. Noxell said it would use a new nonanimal test for its skin creams and cosmetics.

Another major victory occurred when the H. J. Heinz Company agreed that its Star Kist subsidiary would no longer purchase tuna caught in nets that endanger the lives of dolphins. In 1988 Earth Island Institute hired a small advertising agency in San Francisco that specializes in telling consumers what they should not buy for ethical and social reasons. The Public Media Center ran a series of full-page ads in the *New York Times* and the *Wall Street Journal* urging consumers to boycott Heinz because of the "dolphin massacre." Though there was no evidence that the boycott hurt Heinz's sales, the $250,000 ad campaign contributed to the company's decision to give in on April 16, 1990. Several other large tuna companies immediately announced similar plans to purchase tuna only from fishermen using dolphin-safe nets and methods, though by late 1990 only Heinz appeared to be living up to this promise, according to the Earth Island Institute.

WOMEN AND SRI

It is interesting to note that women scientists and entrepreneurs have been particularly active in the animal rights movement. In 1982 Dr. Virginia Gordon began researching alternatives to animal testing, which is often painful and stressful to the animal. For example, after World War II the Draize method was developed to test the eye irritancy of products, particularly cosmetics. This method involved placing a small amount of a substance into a rabbit's eye and checking them for cloudness—a possible indication of irritation. The test takes around twenty-one days to complete, and it depends upon highly subjective judgments by those testing the animals. As a result of her research, Dr. Gordon invented and trademarked the EYTEX. This in vitro (test-tube) method uses a machine to analyze the effect of a substance on a special matrix of vegetable protein that mimics the response of the human cornea. In 1985 she and several other scientists founded a company to produce the EYTEX method and research other alternatives to animal testing. EYTEX is used by around sixty U.S. companies, including Avon, Gillette, and Tom's of Maine.

Lillian Menasche was born in Leipzig, Germany, in 1927, and ten years later her family moved through Holland to the United States to escape nazism. In 1951 she began a small home-based mail-order business offering personalized purses and belts. Three years later the line was expanded to include combs, blazer buttons, collar pins, and cuff links, and Lillian Vernon designed a sixteen-page black-and-white brochure that was mailed to 125,000 customers. Her company also began manufacturing custom-designed products for such firms as Max Factor, Elizabeth Arden, Avon, and Revlon. By 1988 the Lillian Vernon Corporation was mailing eleven catalog editions to 101 million people and doing more than $126 million in total sales annually.

When the company's customers complained, Lillian Vernon did not hesitate to drop some fur and ivory products from its inventory and to establish a policy that no such products would be carried in the future. The company also has other special social

attributes. Portions of a sale of a stuffed panda bear were donated
to the World Wildlife Fund, and imported items come from more
than thirty 30 countries—but not from South Africa. Lillian Vernon also selects third world crafts made by artisans from under-
developed countries, and profits from the sale of terry-cloth robes
were donated to the Retinitis Pigmentosa Foundation. Women
have equal representation on the company's management team.
Employees do not jeopardize their positions during pregnancy
leaves, and on-site health benefits have included breast and skin
cancer screening, hypertension testing, exercise and weight control programs, and first-aid training.

In her baggy shirts and battered ankle boots, Anita Roddick,
founder of The Body Shop, is hardly the archetype for the successful entrepreneur. She doesn't even like to talk about cosmetics, the things that have contributed to her personal wealth of
$200 million. Yet Roddick is the fourth-richest woman in Great
Britain, has been made an officer of the Order of the British
Empire by the queen, and was named "Businesswoman of the
Year" in Britain for 1985.

Anita Roddick would much rather talk about saving rain forests and helping the third world with economic trade. Her cosmetic products, which she began mixing on her kitchen table
fourteen years ago, are sold in stores around the world, including
21 stores in the United States. Another hundred new stores in
the United States are planned for the future. All the products are
made from natural ingredients, and they are not tested on animals. The shops do not advertise and do not make exaggerated
claims about beauty. In addition to the products, the stores are
filled with free-of-charge educational literature about animal rights
and environmentalism. It is this socially responsible commitment plus word-of-mouth publicity that has accounted for The
Body Shop's stunning success. As one British analyst told *Newsweek*, the company's shares of stock did "defy gravity" in a British
economy that had been generally depressed.

Despite these success stories, women still face problems in
business, including the so-called glass ceiling—practices and
prejudices that keep women from achieving the highest executive

positions. A 1987 study of forty-three consumer products companies by the Council on Economic Priorities and commissioned by *Ms.* magazine disclosed that many companies tend to be standouts only in some areas of women's issues while being poor in others. For example, Avon had an outstanding rating for women among officials and managers (more than 81 percent) but a very poor rating for benefits such as flextime or maternal leave. Eastman Kodak had innovative benefits such as six-months' unpaid leave for adoption and unpaid leave for sick-child care but fewer than 8 percent women officials and managers.

In a 1988 book on *The Best Companies for Women* the authors, Baila Zeitz and Lorraine Dusky, identified 50 companies of 198 studied as the ones with the best records for responding to women's issues in the workplace. They found that the single most important factor in determining whether or not women were treated fairly was the person at the top of the company. Not surprisingly, Barrios Technology and Drake Business Schools made the fifty best list because they both were started by women. However, the top men at Fidelity Bank, Gannett Company, Payless Cashways, Pitney Bowes, the *Denver Post* and U S West all were cited as having progressive attitudes toward hiring, training, and promoting women to the highest positions.

Studies such as GOOD MONEY Publications' "Annual Subscriber Survey" have suggested that women might well constitute a significant majority of all those actively involved in the SRI movement. In 1990, 86 percent of all personal wealth in the United States was controlled by women, and 61 percent of all family bills were paid by women. Partly because three-quarters of all married women outlive their husbands, 62 percent of all shareholders were women. It has long been known that women come to business and investing without the traditional male belief that mixing ethics with financial decisions is bad for business and investments. Together with widespread public concern about energy and the environment, the increasing participation of women in business and financial activities has helped fuel SRI.

8

SRI INTERNATIONAL

By 1990 it was apparent that the time had also come for SRI throughout the world, particularly in Europe. Several things accounted for this. National economic barriers were disappearing as localized economies became globalized. Increasing numbers of U.S. companies were developing business and economic ties with foreign businesses, both within the United States and overseas. In April 1990 the *New York Times* reported that there were strong pressures, especially from large institutional investors, to develop a pan-European stock market, which would trade the stocks of Europe's biggest companies.

At the same time there was growing recognition throughout the world that major social problems, such as environment pollution, do not respect national boundaries. The journal of the Federation of American Scientists reported that by late 1985 more than 100,000 gallons of hazardous waste from Southern California had found its way to an open field in Tecate, Mexico, assisted by bribes to Mexican customs agents. In another case, 275 drums of dangerous wastes, falsely labeled as "cleaning fluids," were purchased by a company in Zimbabwe using federal funds from the U.S. Agency for International Development. While an agency audit was disclosing the scam, about 1,500 gallons of dangerous waste remained unmonitored in a phosphate pit in that country.

Both the globiliazation of the economy and the global impact of social problems require social investors to take into account the foreign connections of their investments. There are both indirect and direct ways in which U.S. investors can participate in foreign investments. In addition, there are a growing number of foreign resources to help investors monitor the economic and social features of international investments.

FOREIGN OPPORTUNITIES FOR SOCIAL INVESTORS

Nothing symbolized the globalization of economic markets as much as Mikhail Gorbachev's dramatic announcement in 1987 that Soviet law would be changed to permit joint ventures with foreign companies. Until *perestroika*, business collaborations with the Soviet Union had been limited to the direct sale of goods and services or complex barter agreements. The Soviet attitude had been: "We don't need or want outside help." By 1988 some forty agreements had been initiated with American companies, though most of the ventures were struggling to succeed. Canadian-based Phargo Management had opened a copying center on Gorky Street in Moscow, and the Sony Corporation announced it would join Visa International and PepsiCo as the first foreign advertisers to buy commercial time on Soviet television.

Investors, then, can invest in U.S. companies developing foreign ties. In 1990 the *New York Times* reported that Ben & Jerry's Homemade was working on one of the most unusual joint ventures. The idea came from David Kelley, a Montpelier, Vermont, attorney, and the director of Project Harmony, a cultural exchange program for high school choral groups. He mentioned to Ben Cohen that raising money to pay for exchanges was a continual problem. B&J's proposed that the company open ice-cream parlors in a Moscow shopping mall. The proceeds would remain in a currency account in the Soviet Union to be used to support student exchanges. In addition, the ice cream would be made from Russian agricultural products.

Investors can also select U.S. companies with good social records in their foreign operations. By 1980 the Massachusetts-based Norton Company was an international manufacturer of abrasives and a variety of industrial products, and the company considered itself a "global" rather than a "multinational" corporation. In 1981 Norton developed a set of guidelines, assisted by its Corporate Ethics Committee, for responsible management and personnel policies in diverse foreign cultures. Also in the early 1980s, Norton spent $3.7 million on health and safety improvements in its plants around the world. The company's plants provided good working conditions for employees, including medical and dental care.

Investors can also invest directly in foreign securities. There are prudent economic reasons for doing so. In his 1985 book *How to Buy Foreign Stocks and Bonds*, Gerald Warfield points out that portfolio security can sometimes be enhanced by diversification into foreign stocks and bonds. This means that an investor's fortunes are not being bet only on what happens to U.S. markets or industries. In 1974 U.S. securities represented almost 75 percent of the world's capitalization. By 1985, Warfield reports, this portion had dropped to around 55 percent. In addition, increasing numbers of foreign companies were becoming major players in the world's markets by manufacturing needed products for the world's developing economies. For example, by the 1980s the Matsushita Electric Industrial Company, Japan's largest maker of consumer electronic and electrical goods, had begun producing solar-powered household equipment (such as direct-current VCRs, typewriters, and telephone answering machines) for consumers in regions of the world not served by utility-generated power.

Some foreign opportunities are easily available to U.S. investors. As the earlier example of Volvo indicated, some foreign companies trade on the U.S. stock exchanges in American depository receipts (ADRs). Volvo is listed on the New York Stock Exchange, while automaker Jaguar and news service Reuters

Holdings are listed on the NASDAQ (National Association of Securities Dealers Automated Quotations) market. ADRs are printed and issued by a depository bank in cooperation with a custodian bank (usually a foreign correspondent bank) that purchases stock on a foreign exchange and puts it into its custody. The ADRs represent the foreign shares of stock. A U.S. investor can buy or sell ADRs in the same manner as U.S. stock shares. In addition, holders of ADRs can transfer the U.S. receipts for the underlying foreign shares of stock. Dividends on the stocks underlying ADRs are received by the depository bank, which passes the proceeds in U.S. dollars on to U.S. holders, less foreign withholding taxes. The foreign correspondent bank informs the U.S. bank about exchange offers, annual shareholder meeting dates, and any other information of importance to the U.S. ADR holders.

In an article on ADRs for the journal of the American Association of Individual Investors in 1987, Alan Tucker pointed out that in 1961 there were only 150 ADR opportunities available for U.S. investors. By 1987 more than 600 ADRs existed on all three U.S. American stock exchanges, and these represented the stocks of companies from sixteen different countries. In 1985 ADR trading volume was $9.83 billion, with 912 million shares traded. By 1986 the volume had jumped to $20 billion, with 1.6 billion shares traded. ADR trading is crucial for some foreign companies. For example, ADR trading accounted for 46 percent of the market in Jaguar's shares. The London Stock Exchange also began trading ADRs in August 1987.

Modern telecommunications has made it easier to initiate direct trades on foreign stock markets. However, the benefits of direct international diversification of investments can be mitigated by political and exchange rate risks. In addition, there are sometimes institutional barriers. The sale and settlement of shares of foreign stock are often more difficult because they are usually issued in bearer form, rather than in registered form, as in the case of U.S. securities. What this means is that the bearer or the possessor is considered the owner, and the certificates come with attached coupons for interest or dividends that must be presented for payment. When sold, bearer securities must be physically delivered to the purchaser. Owners of registered securities, however, can store them anywhere, dividends and interest are paid automatically, and when a security is sold, all that needs to be done is change the registered name of the owner. Still, after all is said and done, Tucker found that an international portfolio of fifty stocks invested in seven major stock markets in the world was significantly less risky than a U.S. portfolio of similar size.

Finally, though community-oriented banking is not as developed in Europe as it is in the United States, some opportunities began to appear by 1990. Large German banks (Deutsche Bank, Dresdner Bank, and Commerzbank) expressed no interest in ethical investing. However, some small banks in that country operated on what was called anthropocentric principles—principles that lead to business practices that respect and uphold human values. The Bank für Sozialwirtschaft (Bank for a Social Economy), GLS Gemeinschaftsbank eG (Community Bank), and Öko-Bank were examples. All provided or were planning social equity or bond funds.

The typical social fund in Germany for the small investor required a minimum deposit of DM5,000 (about $3,000 at the mid-1990 exchange rate). Since social information about continental European companies was still not extensive, investments in British companies were often relied upon. Investments were paid into a trust center and then distributed initially among British ethical funds, such as the Stewardship Trust and Merlin Ecology Trust.

Like Chicago's South Shore, Öko-Bank was a very atypical bank. It was founded in 1988 by peace activists, and its managers wore blue jeans and gym shoes and sat in wicker chairs. There was no environmentally unsound plastic in the office, and all deposit and withdrawal slips and handouts were printed on recycled paper. From 1988 to mid-1989 almost 19,000 people opened more than 26,000 accounts, and the bank's equity base grew 62 percent to DM9.7 million (about $5.8 million), while the balance sheet surged to almost DM50 million (about $30 million). The bank was owned by 15,500 cooperative shareholders, who held an average of DM600 (about $360) in non-interest-paying capital. Öko-Bank funded projects that traditional banks would not consider and that supported education, ecology, psychiatry, cooperative businesses, and women's groups. Similar to the Vermont National Bank, Öko-Bank also guaranteed that depositors' money would not support South African apartheid, weapons work, or environmental pollution.

HOW FOREIGN SRI PAYS OFF

By 1988 some British organizations involved with SRI were beginning to develop and report on studies of the financial impact of making social decisions for investment purposes. The *Ethical Investor*, published by the Ethical Investment Research Service (EIRIS) in London, described a report by a senior vice-president for BARRA International (a financial analysis firm) at a conference on ethical investing. BARRA conducted a five-year study (from October 1983 to October 1988) of the performance of eight portfolios with different types of social screens compared with the market as a whole. Performance was measured by dividend yield and capital appreciation. Three separate South Africa-free portfolios were designed to avoid companies with any involvement in that country, to screen out companies in South Africa with more than a thousand employees, and to screen out companies in South Africa paying unacceptably low wages. In addition, the research looked at portfolios that were arms-free (nuclear weapons), financial-free (banks and insurance companies), nuclear power-free, and tobacco-free (large-scale involvement and production). Finally, these seven portfolios were combined to create an eighth portfolio, which reflected all these social concerns.

By October 1988, the dividend yield for all seven of BARRA's ethically screened portfolios combined was 4.38 percent, compared with a yield of 4.36 percent for an all-share, unscreened index. (While a 0.02 percent difference may seem small, over the long term, the compounded gain can be quite significant.) The best performer was the tobacco-free portfolio with a yield of

4.79 percent, followed by the nuclear-free at 4.77 percent, financial-free at 4.61 percent, and arms-free at 4.58 percent. One South Africa-free portfolio (low pay) was higher than the combined and market averages at 4.47 percent yield. Two were lower—more than a thousand employees at 4.34 percent and any involvement in South Africa at 4.08 percent. In other words, six of the eight screened portfolios had higher yield performances than the market as a whole.

In capital appreciation, the South Africa-free portfolio, which screened for any involvement, outperformed the index by 0.03 percent per month, or around 2 percent cumulatively over the five years. BARRA found that four of its ethical portfolios performed slightly better than the index, while the other four performed slightly worse. The conclusion was that ethical constraints on investments do not appear, on the whole, to lead to any measurable difference between the performance of ethically screened portfolios compared with unscreened investments. The most important factor in performance was the financial strategy of the investment manager, not the presence or absence of social constraints. For example, for the four-year period ending January 6, 1989, the first British ethical fund increased 196 percent compared with a 95 percent increase for the DJIA.

Some foreign opportunities for U.S. investors have done spectacularly well. Consider the examples of some Japanese companies, available to U.S. investors through ADRs. They can be attractive to socially concerned investors, since many make useful and high-quality products, and Japanese companies have no large national defense-spending exposure. Cooperation among business, labor, and government characterizes Japanese industry. The much-touted Japanese managerial style does create a context within which employee needs are seen to have central concern, and Japanese firms use quality circles (teams of workers who play an active role in the production process), stress job training and promotion, and make it possible for a worker to rise from the shop floor to the executive suite. Indeed, the Japanese boss's son must start on the shop floor to reach the executive suite. These factors may be some of the reasons why the recent performance for the ADRs of some Japanese companies has been truly impressive. From the end of 1980 through 1989 the DJIA rose 186 percent while the GMIA jumped 323 percent. For the same period of time the combined ADRs of six Japanese companies making much-needed products rose almost 490 percent (not including dividends paid), as the table below shows. All the companies outperformed the DJIA, and only one (TDK) performed below the GMIA.

In 1988 the *Wall Street Journal* reported that at a time when big U.S. airlines were trying to dominate and monopolize markets through hostile take-overs and ruthless competition, a growing number of foreign air carriers had discovered a better idea: cooperation. These foreign airlines wanted to grow in order to be able to compete with huge U.S. airlines, and for a time they followed the U.S. competitive model. However, the different laws, regulations, and currency restrictions applying in each country made this difficult. Instead, foreign companies began talking about such things as joint marketing and operational alliances, shared

		End of 1980 to End of 1989 Change In	
JAPANESE COMPANY	PRODUCTS	AVERAGE YEARLY ADR PRICE	DIVIDENDS
Fuji Photo	Photo film and paper, cameras, lenses, video / audiocassettes	+994%	+139%
Matsushita Electric	Video, TVs, industrial communications, home appliances	+552	+103
Canon, Inc.	Copiers, single-lens reflex cameras, typewriters, computers, calculators, video camcorders	+443	+139
Pioneer Electric	Home / car audio, videodiscs, TVs, telephone answering machines	+439	+50
Sony Corp.	Video, audio, TVs, semiconductors	+407	+143
TDK Corp.	Ferrites, video / audiotape, TVs, VCRs	+270	+233
All six companies		*+ 489%*	*+121%*

flight codes, joint purchase agreements, and minority equity swaps. Some of the foreign airlines involved in these cooperative negotiations were:

Aerolineas Argentinas
Air New Zealand
Alitalia
British Airways
KLM Royal Dutch Airlines
Koninklijke Nedlloyd Groep N.V. (a Dutch shipping company which owned two air carriers, Netherlines and Transavia)
Sabena (Belgium)
Scandinavian Airlines System
Swissair
Union de Transports Aériens (France)

KLM can be purchased by investors in U.S. shares of stock on the NYSE. From the end of 1980 through 1989 KLM's revenues grew 108 percent, the company's net profit soared more than 3,000 percent, and the average annual stock price for the U.S. shares climbed 260 percent.

A truely remarkable and profitable example of successful cooperation can be found in the Basque region of Spain. In 1956 Ulgor (a worker cooperative) with twenty-three employees opened its doors in Mondragón to make electrical and mechanical products for home use. Just three decades later this business was part of a complex of worker-owned cooperatives employing almost twenty thousand people in more than over 100 worker cooperatives and supporting organizations. These cooperatives and organizations provided educational, industrial research, and banking services in addition to being involved in agricultural and industrial production. Of the 103 worker cooperatives created from 1956 to 1986, only 3 had closed. Therefore, after five years of opening, 97 percent of the new cooperative firms were in operation. In the United States, after 5 years of opening, only 20 percent of new cooperative firms are in operation. One of the problems in the United States is the conflict between the employee as shareholder and the employee as democratic participant in the operation of the firm. In other words, the desire to benefit socially can come into conflict with the desire to profit financially, thereby undermining the ability of the cooperative to succeed financially or to maintain its cooperative ideals.

The success of the Mondragón cooperative complex, from the 1950s to the mid-1980s, is even more remarkable when one realizes that the cooperatives had to deal with economic stagnation and inflation in the Spanish economy in the 1970s. In 1972 one study found that cooperative efficiency in Spain exceeded the efficiency of the largest enterprises by 7.5 percent and of medium-size and small companies by 40 percent. In a 1980s worldwide recession Spain was particularly hard hit, but Mondragón continued doing very well. According to a study by William Foote Whyte and Kathleen King Whyte in 1988, this financial success was a result of a spirit of cooperation throughout the cooperative, in contrast with the spirit of domination that often characterizes more traditional business firms. This spirit was enhanced by a structure of autonomous work divisions and organizations, which shared goods and services. The nonhierarchical structure encouraged horizontal rather than vertical relationships—ones of equality rather than inequality.

During the 1980s more traditionally organized foreign companies were also profitably experimenting with a variety of innovative social programs and policies. In Finland the forestry and paper company Enso Gutzeit sold its tree harvesters and tractors to their operators, with preferential loan terms, and helped them begin operating as independent subcontractors. The result was a 30 percent increase in annual working loads. Finland's Tammerneon, makers of neon light, turned employees into their own company. The employees rented their old work space and machinery and bought materials from the former employer. According to Tammerneon's managing director, the industrial relations climate improved and productivity rose 250 percent.

In Spain the printer Artes Graficas sold a majority ownership to its fifty-three employees. Within a year profits had reached 60 percent of the capital invested, while the order book became full. The work generated by the former company, which it had had difficulty handling, was taken care of by only eighteen workers, leaving the rest free to deal with new outside business. In Great Britain the chemicals company ICI had been spinning off computer programmers, gardeners, photographers, and others with special skills as independent contractors. During the first year the fledgling entrepreneurs were taught the skills of small business, given practical help by ICI, and guaranteed a salary equivalent to the previous year's earnings. In some cases the former employees received a contract to provide specific services to ICI. As of 1983, all the spin-offs had been successful.

State-owned French chemicals maker Rhône-Poulenc had been having severe operating problems as a result of being caught with some obsolete plants at the beginning of a recession in the European economy. The company was particularly sensitive to the acute problems created in communities when factories were closed down. Local employment in some cases had been cut by up to one-third with no prospects for alternative work. In response, Rhône-Poulenc created a subsidiary, SOPRAN (Société pour la Promotion d'Activités Nouvelles). SOPRAN's primary function was to attract other companies to the communities that Rhône-Poulenc had left. By 1983 some twenty-five hundred jobs had been created, eight hundred of them for former Rhône-Poulenc employees. SOPRAN provided inexpensive premises on the sites of the old factories and helped train the new work force. For example, Intermagnetics, an electronics company needing room for expansion, was located on a former Rhône-Poulenc site at Besançon, and Intercassettes, a videocassette company, moved into Montluçon. A small fine chemicals and pharmaceuticals company was persuaded to move from cramped quarters in Paris to a former Rhône-Poulenc site in Lyons.

SOPRAN also used its resources to seek out new products that had been shelved because they did not represent a big enough market for a large global firm. For example, one venture involved helping a group of young entrepreneurs in Cambrai to develop crop-spraying techniques using ultralight monoplanes, instead of fuel-hungry conventional planes or helicopters. Rhône-Poulenc benefited in these cases when the small company became either a user or supplier of its products. The company won praise throughout Europe for its community concern. As a result, banks were willing to finance restructuring programs, and the French government gave Rhône-Poulenc favored treatment with regard to investment.

By 1984 increasing numbers of German companies were discovering that the greater the freedom they gave their employees to work when they wanted to, the higher the productivity they achieved. Indeed, the concept of flextime was first implemented in Germany's Messerschmitt airplane factories. Basically, at regular periods of six months or a year, employees were given the chance to decide how many hours they wanted to work during the coming year. At Munich's famous Beck-Feldmeier store, the nine hundred employees had a range of options from full-time work (about 2,000 hours per year) down to 720 hours in stages of 120 hours each. Matching an employee's choice with business needs was facilitated by computer information that accurately predicted the peaks and valleys for all departments, by season, by day of the week and by time of the day. The company operated an "hours bank" with some people in credit and others in debit. Most employees preferred to build up a credit in order to use it at convenient times (when the children were on vacation). As a result of flextime, the Munich store reported substantial increases in sales per employee-hour, while labor costs dropped. So popular had the practice become that two-thirds of the employees were working one of the part-time options, and the caliber of the staff had increased. For example, many mothers who had not considered working in a store were attracted by the flexible part-time options.

CAUTIONS FOR U.S. INVESTORS
GOING FOREIGN

As the previous discussion of foreign investment opportunities has indicated, U.S. investors considering going foreign should be aware of special economic and social risks. Critics have pointed out that rampant speculation can easily influence foreign markets and economies, and it is often difficult for U.S. investors to measure the impact of this on foreign investments. Again, consider the case of Japan. Before the international stock market crashes in 1987, one share of Nippon Telephone was selling at $20,000, and the average P / E ratio for Japanese stocks was more than 60—a level considered extremely risky for a U.S. stock. In 1987 there were other signs of trouble ahead as well. A Japanese golf club membership could cost up to $750,000, and an insurance company paid $40 million for a van Gogh painting. One renter paid $19,000 per month for a three-bedroom apartment, and a store owner committed suicide when the assessed value of his leased land was raised to $55,000 per square meter ($261 per square foot). In 1987 the Japanese stock market Nikkei Average of 225 stocks peaked at 26,646, before plunging to a bottom of 19,532.

U.S. analysts were in disagreement about what all this meant. In retrospect, the 27 percent drop in the Nikkei Average didn't look all that bad. In the final quarter of 1987 the average declined only 17 percent, compared with a 25 percent loss for the DJIA and a 26 percent loss for London's *Financial Times* Industrial Average. In addition, for the first two months of 1988 the Nikkei Average rose 15 percent, compared with a 2.5 percent and 1.2 percent rise for the other two averages respectively. Some analysts pointed out that the long tradition whereby the Japanese government closely works with the Japanese financial community creates greater stability than in other economies, particularly during rocky periods. Others argued that Japanese government and brokers were involved in a conspiracy to push up Japanese stock-prices beyond reasonable levels (thus the extremely high P / E ratios). They pointed out that this was one reason why, by early 1988, foreigners had accounted for only 3 percent of the capitalization of the Tokyo Stock Exchange, compared with more than 8 percent three years earlier. Too, by early 1988 only 1 percent of U.S. pension fund assets were invested in Japanese stocks.

It is also important to monitor foreign companies closely for practices that differ from U.S. corporations. When U.S. companies started pulling out of South Africa, Japanese companies (such as Nissan and Toyota) rushed in to fill the void. In 1987 Japan's trade with South Africa amounted to more than $4 billion, a jump of more than 14 percent from the previous year. U.S. 1987 South Africa trade was less than $3 billion. Though the international community expressed misgivings, there was no great public outcry in Japan—a society that does not have a black and white racial problem. (Japan is not without its own racial problems. Koreans and the Ainus of northeastern Japan have experienced discrimination. The Ainus, white Japanese who are believed to have been the first people to have lived in Japan, have a similar relationship to the larger Japanese population as Native Americans in the United States. Ainus live in separate communities, and the Japanese have tried to suppress their language, religion, and customs.) The treatment of blacks is not seen as a high-priority issue in Japan. Nevertheless, in 1987 *Business Week* reported that some Japanese politicians and activists admitted embarrassment about the willingness of their corporations to do business in an apartheid state and were afraid that it might make it look as though Japan were indifferent to injustice.

As difficult as it may be for concerned investors and consumers to assess the social aspects of foreign companies, it is becoming more and more imperative. One reason is international mergers and buyouts. In 1980 the *Financial Times* reported that Britain's Barclays Bank had taken over six U.S. banks between 1968 and 1980. In addition, Lloyds took over one in 1973; Midland, two between 1973 and 1980; National Westminster, one in 1979; and Standard Chartered, one in 1980. By mid-1988 about four dozen California wineries and vineyards, including several of the largest and best known, were foreign-owned or had foreign investors. Otsuka Pharmaceuticals (Japan) owned Ridge Vineyards, A. Rake (Germany) owned the Buena Vista Winery, and Four Seas Investing (Thailand) owned Domaine St. George. By mid-1988 Firestone Tire and Rubber had reached an agreement to sell most of its tire operations to Japan's Bridgestone Corporation and General Mills had sold a piece of Betty Crocker to foreigners.

The question of jobs for U.S. workers has also troubled some analysts for both economic and social reasons. There is a feeling that Japanese, South African, or German employers are less likely to care about the preservation of jobs in the United States than U.S. employers. The issue of foreign products is also involved. In 1982 *Industry Week* estimated that in the previous year more than 400,000 Americans had lost jobs because of foreign automobile imports. Toyota shot back by arguing that it alone had created more than 35,000 jobs in dealerships, at its U.S. headquarters, for independent distributors, and for longshoremen and other workers.

On the morning of March 16, 1990, Norton Company executives woke up to discover that a hostile tender offer of $75 per share had been made by the British conglomerate BTR p.l.c. What made this offer so disturbing was Norton's record for outstanding corporate citizenship and BTR's reputation for buying up companies and dismantling them for the profits to be made. During the following month Norton's employees organized protest demonstrations, a bill was introduced into the Massachusetts legislature in an attempt to make take-overs in the state more difficult, and Norton's board flatly rejected BTR's offer as inadequate. Since Norton's annual meeting of shareholders was scheduled to take place almost immediately, all these moves appeared to be no more than symbolically important. Norton's CEO went looking for a "white knight"—someone who could outbid BTR, take over Norton, and promise to keep the company financially and socially intact.

On April 24 Norton announced it had found its savior in the Paris-based Compagnie de Saint-Gobain. The French conglomerate offered to pay $90 a share for Norton and, in a move unique to take-overs, promised to continue Norton's charitable contributions at their current level for five years, to keep the Norton name and Worcester, Massachusetts, headquarters, and to maintain employment policies and employee benefits at existing levels. John Nelson, Norton's CEO, commented: "We feel very good about this—particularly because Saint-Gobain has a track record of living up to the same kinds of commitments at CertainTeed

Company in Valley Forge, which they acquired some six to eight years ago."

There was an interesting financial footnote to this case. When BTR made its first offer to shareholders, it was very tempting to jump at the offering price. Norton's stock had been trading around $55 a share just before the offer. The $75 sale price represented an overnight capital gain of 36 percent. However, because a number of Norton's shareholders resisted the BTR buy-up on social grounds, the eventual offer from Saint-Gobain represented a 67 percent gain.

FOREIGN SRI ADVISERS

The Toronto-based Taskforce on the Churches and Corporate Responsibility (TCCR) issues reports on socially screened funds available in Canada. These include the Environmental Investment Canadian Fund / Environmental Investment International Fund (no minimum deposit), Ethical Growth Fund (minimum deposit of Canadian $100), Canadian Ethical / Dynamic / Responsible Fund (C.E.D.A.R.—minimum deposit of Canadian $250,000), Crown Commitment Fund (managed by a life insurance company—minimum deposit of Canadian $100), and Investors Summa Fund Ltd. (minimum deposit of Canadian $1,000). All these funds screen for military weapons; four screen for environmental programs and practices; and three screen for employee relations, nuclear energy, and trade with oppressive regimes. According to TCCR, the Environmental Fund had the most extensive screen with ten criteria; Crown had nine; C.E.D.A.R., seven; Summa, five; and Ethical two. Among other screens included are the old sin screen (Summa), product quality (Crown and Environmental), South Africa (Crown), philanthropic programs (Crown), and truthful advertising (Crown).

At the March 14, 1988, quarterly meeting of the Social Investment Forum in Boston, John Jordan, vice-president for planning and development of the Co-Operators Insurance Company of

Ontario, explained the basic differences between SRI in Canada and the United States. On the positive side, the Canadian government, both Conservative and Liberal, has played a very direct role in the economy and in responding to social issues. Also, cooperatives play a major role in the Canadian economy. One-third of Canadian households are credit union members, and 50,000 families live in co-op housing. On the negative side, the Canadian stock market is smaller, so the limiting of investment opportunities by using social screens does have some impact upon return. Mining makes up 30 percent of all stocks, and distilling, brewing, and tobacco companies also predominate. This is a compelling reason for Canadian investors to internationalize their portfolios, especially with the securities of U.S. companies, where there are many socially acceptable alternatives.

In 1990 the Social Investment Organization, a nonprofit educational group, was formed in Canada to promote ethical and alternative investing. In that year the Vancouver City Savings Credit Union added environmental and tobacco screens to its popular Ethical Growth Fund, which had assets of more than Canadian $36 million (more than U.S. $31 million by mid-1990 exchange rates). In addition, Eugene Ellmen, author of a book about ethical investing in Canada, announced plans to begin publishing a newsletter for Canadian social investors: the *Conscientious Investor.*

Australia is another English-speaking country where SRI appears to be rapidly spreading. In early 1989 the MoneyMatters Financial Group was formed to provide complete financial services for investors concerned about the impact of their investments on communities, the environment, and society at large. By 1990 the North Coast Ethical Credit Union provided members with screens for pollution of the environment, violations of human rights, the manufacture of armaments, and discrimination on the basis of sex, race, creed, disability, or income. North Coast not only avoided loans to businesses or activities with these problems but also sought out businesses and activities that had a positive environmental and social impact.

Three socially screened Australian funds were also available.

The YWCA Ethical Investment Trust was managed to reflect the philosophical and ethical concerns of the Young Women's Christian Association. Of particular importance were environmental, health, education, and human rights issues. Minimum investment was Australian $1,000 (about U.S. $806). The August Investments Managed Trust advertised itself as an ethical investment fund that grew trees, built houses, promoted recycling, and empowered employees to own their workplaces. Minimum investment was Australian $1,000. A more comprehensive environmental fund was the Occidental Environmental Opportunities Fund. This fund sought out investments in recycling, waste management, pollution controls, public transportation, energy- and resource-efficient housing, eucalypt afforestation, and environmentally benign products.

A country where SRI could experience great growth in the near future is Germany. Of central concern in that country are environmental pollution and related issues, such as nuclear power and weapons makers. In 1989 *Manager Magazine*, an influential German monthly for executives, reported that though thirty-five-year-old Bonn investment consultant Robert Schneider had successfully pursued a conventional career, he was troubled. Personally he opposed the apartheid policies in South Africa, environmental pollution, and nuclear rearmament. However, his profession required him to invest the capital of his clients in these things. Schneider wanted to quit his job until he discovered the successes of SRI in the English-speaking financial world.

In December 1988 Schneider, together with Albert Eskenazy and Eberhard Scholl, founded Gesellschafter der ARTUS Ethische Vermögensverwaltung (ARTUS Ethical Portfolio Management Company). Its purposes include making SRI known in Germany, marketing ethical mutual funds, establishing an ethical research center, and creating an archive on ethical investment. The articles of the company state that ARTUS is an "investment medium for investors that do not consider financial profit to be the sole criterion for investment." By mid-1989 Schneider and Eskenazy reported that they were overwhelmed with inquiries. In addition to the article in *Manager Magazine*, the German weekly *Die Zeit* featured ARTUS, as did the *Green Pages 1989*, a directory of German companies that make products that do not harm the environment.

By October 1989 ARTUS reported that it had joined with Concorde to develop and market an ethical savings plan. Concorde was a financial organization with more than a thousand intermediaries and fifty offices in Germany and Austria. Within the first ten weeks of marketing, some 3,000 savings plans were started. The goal, eventually, was to attract 2,000 new investors per month. As little as DM50 (about U.S. $30 at mid-1990 exchange rate) per month and an initial deposit of only DM1,000 (about $600) could open a plan. The savings plans were pooled into a common account and invested in four British and U.S. ethical funds for a minimum period of twelve years. Starting in 1990, Concorde ceased marketing all the company's other financial products in order to concentrate exclusively upon ethical investing. The prospectus for the savings plan had been translated into English, French, Italian, and Spanish, and Concorde was setting up marketing organizations in France, Italy, Scandinavia, and Spain.

ARTUS also reported that the socially responsible Bank für Sozialwirtschaft was having problems launching the first ethical pension fund in Germany. The Bundesaufsichtsamt für das Kreditwesen (Federal Supervisory Board for Credit) continued to block the creation of social funds that used such terms as *environmental, ethical,* and *alternative.* The problem appeared to be that some famous German companies (such as Deutsche Bank, Mercedes, and Siemens) might wind up being categorized as "bad" by some critical criteria.

By 1989 SRI was beginning in other countries as well. In Belgium Vincent Commenne announced the creation of a research and information service for ethical investing. The service was to begin with clients from two mutual funds investing in local and foreign stocks plus individuals interested in ethical investing. Links had already been established with several U.S. organizations and EIRIS in Britain. Contacts were being established with organizations in Germany and Holland. The service would screen investments in Belgium to avoid companies operating in countries with institutionalized repression, making or marketing weapons, generating nuclear energy, and selling alcohol or tobacco products. On the positive side, the service would look for the stocks of companies that respected life and the social and natural environment; saved planetary resources; improved relationships with employees, suppliers, clients, and shareholders; and manufactured or marketed useful and quality products. The service sought out the same information about U.S. and other foreign companies.

Soren Bergstrom reported that interest in SRI was growing in Sweden among journalists, voluntary organizations, and some banks. What was lacking was adequate research, familiarity with financial institutions, and knowledge of the financial risks that might be involved. As a result, the Responsible Investment Foundation (RIF) was established in 1986. RIF provides criteria for ethical screening, while banks supply the financial criteria. For example, by 1989 AB Svensk Fondforvatning was planning an ethical investment fund together with the Foreningsbankernas bank. Initially, most investments would have to be in non-Swedish companies, since time was needed to collect appropriate information and the small country of Sweden did not provide that many immediately identifiable, socially acceptable investments. RIF was also negotiating with a bank to begin a savings account with an ethical screen.

In early 1989 the First International Symposium on Ethics, the Economy, and Business was held in Paris, France. Two sessions dealt with the moral dimension and its relationship to the economy and making ethical decisions in business and investing. Participants included professors, financiers, industrialists, theologians, and representatives of public agencies and private foundations, including the French Fondation pour les Études de Défense Nationale. The international character of SRI was also reflected in the participation of Brussels's European Business Ethics Network and Rome's Institut International Jacques Maritain. Making presentations were professors from the University of Pennsylvania, Tokyo University, and the University of Groningen in the Netherlands. The conference was the result of several years of work by such people as international financial consultant Louis Deschamps, who was also planning a French-based ethical investment fund.

Some countries were in earlier stages of development for SRI. Christoph Pfluger reported that in the traditional banking country of Switzerland there was not one ethical fund to be found. However, in 1988 Pfluger began his own newsletter, *Die Neue Wirtschaft (The New Economy)*. The purposes of the newsletter were to get readers to discover how they could conduct responsible businesses and to challenge the belief system of conventional economics. Pfluger reported that he was getting about a hundred times more response, in relation to circulation, than he got from publishing articles in one of the major economic newspapers in Switzerland.

In mid-1990 Max Dem reported from Austria plans to develop a research institute similar to EIRIS in Great Britain and the Investor Responsibility Research Center in the United States. The institute would be named Forschungsinstitut für ethische-ökologische Geldanlagen (Research Institute for Ethical and Ecological Investments). Plans were also under way to form a private social investment club named Erster ethisch-ökologischer Investment Klub Austria (First Ethical-Ecological Investment Club of Austria, abbreviated ÖKO-INVEST). The club would begin by purchasing shares of such existing funds as New Alternatives in the United States and the British trust. For the first year the size of the Austrian trust was estimated to become 10 million Austrian schillings (more than $850,000), and the minimum investment was 10,000 schillings ($850). Dem also reported that in June 1990 the Budapest Stock Exchange opened in Hungary.

European social investors have identified two foreign companies as examples of those being considered by the new European socially screened funds. Générale des Eaux is a French water management and construction company that is developing a waste water oxidation process. Leffers AG is a German textile company that does not use animal fur in its products.

All the growing foreign activity with socially responsible business practices and investing and the developing links to U.S. counterparts signify the globalization of SRI. Since this trend parallels the globalization of economies, markets, and businesses, it provides an opportunity to bring ethical and moral issues into play with for-profit economic activity on a worldwide basis.

Nothing could be more timely. There is an increasing urgency to bring the world's economic needs into greater harmony with the world's social needs. There is increasing urgency to temper international competition with international cooperation. In a recent book on investing to support the environment, Michael Silverstein, a specialist in environmental economics and finance, quotes British-born poet W. H. Auden when he wrote: "We must love one another or die." Auden was writing about the massive destruction created during World War II. Silverstein concludes by saying: "Today, given the state of the natural environment, it might fairly be said that we must love *everything* or die."

9

AND THE BEAT
GOES ON

Since the first edition of this book was published in 1991, things have steadily been getting better and better for SRI. The performance of socially screened investments has generally been excellent, in many cases much better than traditional unscreened investments. Shareholder action has expanded and become more influential, particularly in the area of environmental protection. More individuals and institutions have become involved in SRI, as demonstrated by the growth in the total net assets and number of investors in the socially screened funds. More corporations have instituted socially responsible programs and practices, and the transglobal influence of SRI is more evident than ever before. This chapter updates some of these more important events in the socially responsible investing movement.

"GOOD DOWS" CONTINUE TO OUTPERFORM WALL STREET'S DOWS

Since the end of 1990, several changes have been made on both the GOOD MONEY Industrial and Utility averages. MCI Communications, Walt Disney, and Wang Laboratories were dropped from the GMIA, as were Kansas Power & Light, Orange & Rockland, and TECO Energy from the GMUA. When the GMIA was first constructed, MCI had been included because it was challenging the virtual monopoly in the U.S. telephone business of AT&T (which appears on the DJIA) and didn't have the social problems associated with AT&T (for example, the Sandia Labs nuclear-weapons work). However, since the spin-off of the "little Bells" from "Ma Bell," some of the former have implemented some very good social programs and practices that MCI does not have. MCI was replaced with US WEST primarily because the latter has an excellent record for the hiring, training, retention, and promotion of women and has been judged by many social analysts to be one of the most "family friendly" companies in America in terms of such practices as parental leave, flextime, and day care.

Since the death of Walt Disney, his company no longer demonstrates the social conscience of its founder. He saw EPCOT Center in Florida as a social experiment in a self-contained, environmentally controlled, domed city of the future. Walt Disney also wanted his company to provide only squeaky-clean family fun. Current Disney executives see the company, and operate it, merely as a giant money machine. Top Disney executives consistently reward themselves with extraordinarily high pay each year—pay that apparently has no connection to company performance. EPCOT now has a bad environmental record and contains entertainment attractions where liquor is available. Because Disney is no longer what its founder envisioned, it was replaced with Blockbuster Entertainment, a video-store chain that advertises itself as operating family-oriented video stores that will not stock X-rated videos.

Since the death of An Wang, Wang Laboratories has fallen on hard economic and social times. For a period of time, An Wang's son badly mismanaged the company. When new management took over, the company was in such financial peril that some of its unusual benefits for employees were scrapped—which explains why it was removed from the GMIA. Wang Labs was replaced by Cummins Engine, a company long known for exceptional employee concern (the company had a no-involuntary-layoff policy, regardless of financial problems, and a strong commitment to the community in which it operates). Finally, as discussed in Chapter 8, when Norton Company was acquired by Compagnie de Saint-Gobain of France, it was necessary to find a substitute on the GMIA. Sallie Mae (Student Loan Marketing Association) was added to provide evidence of a commitment to education on the stock average.

On the GMUA, coal-fired TECO Energy was dropped when it ran into several social problems, including a low S&P rating because of a heavy exposure to possible clean-air costs as a result of a poor environmental record. TECO was replaced with UtiliCorp United (prime fuels are 66 percent coal and 33 percent hydro), a company rated by S&P as having a minimal exposure to clean-air costs because of a good environmental record. Orange & Rockland was dropped when the company signed a five-year agreement to purchase power from Pennsylvania Power & Light Company, which generates about one-third of its power by nuclear energy. The replacement was CILCORP Inc., a coal-fired utility with very high S&P bond ratings because of minimal exposure to clean-air costs. Kansas Power & Light was dropped when the utility acquired Kansas Gas & Electric, a utility with a 47 percent ownership in the troubled Wolf Creek nuclear plant. The replacement was NIPSCO Industries (energy sources: 91 percent coal, 6 percent gas and 3 percent purchased), another company with a high S&P bond rating.

How have these averages been doing through fairly tough economic times? Two recent events rocked the U.S. stock markets—the Persian Gulf War and the fifth-largest one-day drop in the history of the DJIA on November 15, 1991. From August of 1990, when U.S. troops first began to be deployed to Saudi Arabia, to March of 1991, when the fighting stopped, the GMIA was up 8.0 percent compared to a 10.9 percent gain for the DJIA (which contains the stocks of some of the country's largest defense contractors). However, once the hysteria of war and Patriot-missile fever had passed, the GMIA finished 1991 up 28.6 per-

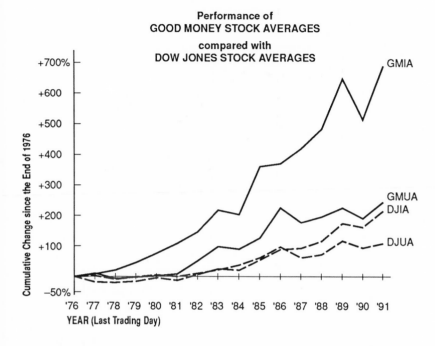

Performance of
GOOD MONEY STOCK AVERAGES
compared with
DOW JONES STOCK AVERAGES

cent compared to a gain of only 20.3 percent for the DJIA for that year. By the end of 1991, the GMIA had a cumulative gain since the end of 1976 of 688.9 percent compared to a cumulative gain for the DJIA of 215.4 percent for the same period. By early 1992, the GMIA's cumulative gain was over 700 percent. For the fifteen-year period, the nuclear-free GMUA was up 244.6 percent compared to a cumulative gain of 108.7 percent for the unscreened DJUA.

On November 15, 1991, the GMIA held ground better than the DJIA in a one-day selling binge, the third such success story (the other two are discussed in Chapter 2) since the inception of the GMIA. On that day, the Dow dropped 3.9 percent while the GMIA fell only 3.1 percent. The performance of the Good Dows through and after the war and the one-day stock market plunge indicated once again the ability of socially screened investments to withstand short-term panic and perform better than profit-only investments over the long term.

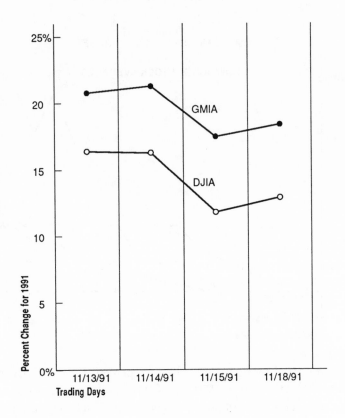

MORE OPPORTUNITIES FOR THE SMALL INVESTOR

Over the last several years, the socially screened funds have continued to grow in number of funds available to investors and in number of investors in the funds. And the funds have continued to prosper. For the year ending on September 30, 1991, the Calvert Social Investment Fund reported a growth in total net assets for its four socially screened portfolios from 1982 (when the first two screened portfolios were offered to the public) of from $2.4 million to $600 million, or almost 25,000 percent in just nine years. From 1990 through 1992, twelve new funds appeared that offered additional opportunities for socially concerned investors:

FUND	TYPE OF FUND
Calvert/Ariel Appreciation Fund	Small company/growth/mutual
Calvert Global Equity Fund	International/mutual
Covenant Portfolio	Income/growth/mutual
Domini Social Index Trust	Income/growth/mutual
Global Environmental Fund, L.P.	Environmental/mutual
Green Century Funds	Money market & balanced/both environmental
GreenEarth Liquid Assets	Environmental fund/income/money market
Merrill Lynch Eco-logical Trust	Environmental/mutual
Muir California Tax-Free Bond Fund	Tax-free/money market
Rightime Social Awareness Fund	Growth/mutual
Shield Progressive Environmental Fund	Environmental/mutual

The Merrill Lynch Eco-logical Trust and Schield's Progressive Environmental Fund both donate a small part of the sales fee to environmental groups. However, two other funds had even a better idea. Green Century Fund is a non-profit organization and gives 100 percent of its net profits away to non-profit environmental and public interest groups. Mindy Lubber, president of the fund, said that the SEC was stunned when they first heard about the proposal. Wall Street never gives anything away to anyone. Not to be outdone, GreenEarth is a money market fund designed for institutional investors. The non-profit Greener Tomorrow Foundation distributes up to 50 percent of the management fee of its investment advisor, New World Advisors, Inc., to environmental groups (or up to twenty-five basis points—0.25 percent—of the fund's total assets). Both of these funds represented new and creative ways of marrying the worlds of for-profit, not-for-profit, and social action.

In 1992, *Business Week* magazine analyzed 760 mutual funds and rated Pax World Fund among their top forty-one performers for risk-adjusted total return to investors. For the years 1982 through 1991, Pax had a ten-year average annual total return, adjusted for risk, of 15.2 percent. Though other funds had higher returns, BW gave Pax a "superior" rating for two reasons—high ideals in terms of its social goals and rarely having a losing year (so that gains in subsequent years are not merely having to make up for losses in prior years). The magazine also gave the Dreyfus Third Century Fund a rating of "superior." Dreyfus had a ten-year average annual return of 13.8 percent adjusted for risk.

For the five-year period ending December 31, 1991, three of the older socially screened funds did especially well compared to the general averages and the averages for all the funds in their category:

| | | 5-Year Return to 12/31/91 | |
FUND	FUND CATEGORY	FOR FUND	FOR AVERAGE
Calvert/Ariel Growth Fund	Small company	+117.2%	
S&P 500			+104.0%
Dreyfus Third Century Fund	Equity/growth	+112.1%	
Equity Funds Average			+89.6%
Small Companies Average			+88.0%
Gen. Growth Funds Average			+86.5%
New Alternatives Fund	Natural resources	+75.4%	
Nat. Res. Funds Average			+47.4%

Part of the good performance for Dreyfus was the fund's managers' successful attempt over the last three years to tighten their social screen. By the end of 1991, almost 30 percent of the fund's net asset value was invested in health care companies. Energy, pollution control, and productive technologies were other important investment areas. This was further proof that social screening can lead to better returns over time.

In early 1990, New York City's Bank for Socially Responsible Lending changed its name to Community Capital Bank of Brooklyn and announced that its initial offering of $6 million in shares was going well. Brooklyn Union Gas, the Episcopal Diocese of Long Island, the Metropolitan Life Insurance Foundation, and the Sisters of St. Joseph of Peace had all been early investors in the new community-oriented bank. By the fall of 1990, the bank completed its stock offering and was awarded its authorization certificate by the New York State Banking Department. The bank officially opened in January of 1991. Like the

South Shore Bank of Chicago, Community Capital is a full-service commercial bank whose main purpose is to make capital available for small business and for the renovation and construction of moderate-income housing in neighborhoods throughout New York City. The bank offers personal and business checking accounts, CDs, and interest-bearing money market accounts. Among the organizations and individuals who received loans and letters of credit in the bank's first year of operation were a nursing home in the South Bronx for AIDS victims and their families, a hardware store in the East Flatbush section of Brooklyn, a construction contractor who is working on affordable housing developments, and a fund to help finance forty units of rehab affordable housing in the Brownsville section of Brooklyn.

Community-based loan funds received a major boost in early 1992 when the Minneapolis-based Community Reinvestment Fund announced that the John D. and Catherine T. MacArthur Foundation had agreed to invest $1 million in CRF's secondary market for community development loans. Nonprofit CRF purchases economic development and affordable housing loans from community-based development organizations and government agencies, pools them together, and issues bonds backed by the loan pool to private investors. By 1992, CRF had provided capital to seventeen community development lenders in four states. It had purchased or contracted to purchase nearly 300 loans totaling more than $3.2 million from the organizations in Illinois, Michigan, Minnesota, and Wisconsin. Plans were underway to begin operations in Washington as well. Based on research by CRF and two other organizations, US WEST published fourteen *Small Business Resources Directories* for the states in which the company provided telecommunications services. In addition, CRF published a *Directory* for the state of Michigan. The *Directories* identify state and local development resources.

Since 1987, The ICA Group (formerly the Industrial Cooperative Association) has been providing the capital of investors in a revolving loan fund to worker-owned and community-based companies. Recipients have included South Bronx-based Cooperative Home Care Associates (employees, mostly women of color, provide care to elders), Chicago's Bethel New Life Recycling Center (a community development corporation), and Maine's John Roberts, Ltd. (a garment manufacturer with 90 percent women employees that was saved from bankruptcy with ICA's help and a worker buyout).

SHAREHOLDER ACTION INCREASES AND BECOMES MORE INFLUENTIAL IN 1991 AND 1992

As opportunities increased for socially concerned investors in the last several years, shareholder action has also grown in numbers of shareholders involved and expanded in terms of the issues concerned investors considered important. In 1991, the Interfaith Center on Corporate Responsibility assisted over 100 of its religious members, four pension funds, four socially responsible investing organizations, seven activist organizations, and seven concerned individuals to sponsor over 350 resolutions at 199 companies. Twenty-nine percent of these shareholder proxies dealt with the issue of American companies doing business in South Africa, and 23 percent dealt with environmental issues. Among the most popular shareholder resolutions were those asking corporate management to sign and adhere to a set of guiding principles—for example, the MacBride Principles for religious equality in Northern Ireland (similar to the Sullivan Principles for racial equality in South Africa), the Valdez Principles for sound environmental practices (drafted by activist groups after Exxon's Alaskan oil spill), and the Maquiladora Report on practices in Mexico (a border region of "free" trade where wages for Mexican workers in U.S. corporations are extremely low and environmental pollution is extremely bad).

The portion of votes that shareholder resolutions received also increased significantly. In 1991, three such resolutions at three corporations actually received a majority of all votes. A resolution asking management to report on environmental principles received over 98 percent of the vote at Chevron; a resolution asking for a report on minority business contractors received over 83 percent of the vote at J. C. Penney; and a resolution asking for a confidential proxy vote received over 54 percent of the votes at AMR Corporation, owners of American Airlines. Similar proxies asking for confidential voting procedures at fourteen other companies received from 33 percent to 50 percent of all votes. It was not uncommon in 1991 for votes on the MacBride Principles or doing business in South Africa to receive from 20 to 30 percent of all the votes.

The Securities & Exchange Commission has traditionally permitted corporations to disallow shareholder resolutions dealing with issues of pay, asserting that these matters were purely business decisions to be made by management alone. However, in 1992, that policy changed dramatically because of increasing public criticism of extraordinarily high pay to top executives, pay that often had no relationship to corporate performance. As most U.S. executives continued to pay themselves very well while many other Americans lost their jobs in a faltering economy, some members of Congress moved to draft legislation curtailing the way executives pay themselves (the most popular and successful device is the stock option). So as not to be outflanked, the SEC reversed its traditional policy and permitted shareholders to sponsor resolutions dealing with pay-related issues. However, SEC regulations stipulated that the results of the voting were to be considered "non-binding" on management. In 1992, pay-related resolutions appeared at ten corporations—Aetna Life & Casualty, Baltimore Gas & Electric, Battle Mountain Gold Company, Bell Atlantic Corporation, Black Hills Corporation, Chrysler Corporation, Eastman Kodak Company, Equimark Corporation, Grumman Corporation, and International Business Machines. The resolutions ranged from pay cuts for board members who did not attend meetings through the elimination of bonuses or retirement plans for executives to the improvement of the disclosure of and justification for compensation of top officers.

Only three of the ten companies (Bell Atlantic, Black Hills, and Baltimore G&E) had stock price gains and earnings increases from 1987 through 1991, and for the most part these increases were modest. One company (Grumman) had an earnings gain for the four-year period of +325.4 percent but a stock price loss of −28.8 percent. The remaining six companies had an average stock price loss of almost −46 percent and an average earnings decline of over 85 percent for the four-year period. It is not surprising that shareholders were concerned about executive pay perks.

ENVIRONMENTALISM TAKES HOLD IN THE 90S

There is no question that issues related to the environment have caught the attention of corporate America in the '90s. Though there was still some corporate flim-flam involved by some companies over the last several years, several others had adopted truly remarkable programs. Though the company had pollution emissions below federal standards, Merck & Company embarked on a program to all but eliminate carcinogenic emissions within two years. One year after the program began, emissions had been cut significantly. Merck also announced plans to minimize drastically any chemical that contributed to environmental problems (such as acid rain), to conduct research into waste minimization and resource conservation, and to implement energy conservation and waste reduction practices.

By 1991, McDonald's had done something quite unique for the corporate world when they permitted representatives of the Environmental Defense Fund to do a complete and uninhibited environmental audit of the company's operations. The result was a long-term environmental plan that was hailed as a model for other companies. It focused upon waste-reduction measures that would influence McD's employees, customers, and principal suppliers (including Coca-Cola, Fort Howard Paper, Georgia-Pacific, James River, Rubbermaid, Stone Container, and Sweetheart Cup).

Since 80 percent of all McD's waste is generated behind the counter, the plan called for the composting of eggshells, coffee grounds, and food scraps. Starch-based material would be tested to replace plastic forks, knives, and spoons. Suppliers must use corrugated boxes that contain at least 35 percent recycled content, and all corrugated boxes will be recycled. Tests were to be conducted for reusable salad lids and shipping pallets, pump-style bulk dispensers for condiments, and refillable coffee mugs. As the plan was being instituted, McD's discovered some unexpected benefits. The quilted, paper-based sandwich wraps that James River developed to replace McD's styrofoam clamshell containers retain heat better, weigh less, cost less to make, and consume less energy to produce. Once again, another company found that it was profitable to be socially responsible.

McD's was not the only one to do so. Several years ago, a Sealtest ice cream plant in Framingham, Massachusetts, was considered a dinosaur not worth continued operation. As the plant aged and the economy slid into a deeper recession, parent company Kraft General Foods tried everything, including cost-cutting and four-day work weeks, but nothing worked. Then the plant's manager asked the Massachusetts Office of Energy Resources to audit the plant for energy efficiency. What resulted was a partnership between the plant, the state, and Boston Edison that saved 180 jobs and created an additional sixty jobs in related energy-efficiency projects. Boston Edison also found that air pollution was reduced because there was less need to generate additional electricity—a need that was the equivalent of the electricity necessary for 1,000 homes a year. Executives at Kraft now tout the plant as a model of economic and environmental success.

Foreign companies also announced major environmental programs. Swissair spent $1.2 million on an environmental audit. One result was a contract with CFM International to build an engine for the airline's Airbus A320s and A321s that reduces the emission of nitrogen oxide by 50 percent. By 1992, the airline had fifty-two orders or options for the Airbuses. Swissair also planned to eliminate disposable tableware on medium- and long-haul flights and plastic tableware on all flights. Plans also included loading fewer meals on European flights, where there were frequently a large number of no-shows, and joint aluminum, glass, and paper recycling with other airlines. When the fewer-meals policy had been in place for just four months, Swissair found that in addition to cutting waste they had already saved the cost of the production and handling of 22,000 meals.

Not everyone had profited from the new environmentalism. Ironically, the companies that have had the toughest time keeping up with rapidly changing environmental demands are the ones in the waste clean-up business, such as Waste Management and Browning-Ferris Industries. In the high-flying 1980s, the stocks of these companies were the darlings of Wall Street, as they climbed continuously to newer and more dizzying heights. Then disaster struck. First, the recession cut down the volume of industrial waste and more companies discovered the economic value of waste-minimization and recycling programs. Second, more communities developed stricter environmental standards for landfills. No longer was it merely a matter of backing a garbage truck up and hauling the whole mess off to a hole in the ground. The total waste stream—recyclables, materials for composting, medical waste, sludge, and solid waste—had to be segmented and managed for special disposal, recycling, or conversion.

After allegations of illegal dumping, restraint of trade, bid-rigging, and insider stock-trading rocked the biggest waste management companies in the late 80s, Browning-Ferris Industries appointed William D. Ruckelshaus as its new CEO. When Ruckelshaus was director of the Environmental Protection Agency in the 1970s, he was known as "Mr. Clean." BFI hoped that he would help polish up the company's tarnished image. In 1991, Ruckelshaus announced a major restructuring which he hoped would enable the company to respond to the new environmental demands. This came none too soon. From 1981 to 1990, BFI's average annual stock price soared over 600 percent before dropping almost 32 percent in 1991. Even more ominous was the fact that while BFI's total revenues grew over 100 percent from 1984 to 1991, the company posted a loss in 1990, and 1991 revenues were almost 63 percent below 1987 revenues.

Other waste-handlers had similar operating problems for some of the same reasons. From 1990 to 1991, Laidlaw's earnings per share dropped over 50 percent, Allwaste's about 34 percent, Chemical Waste Management's around 30 percent, and Chambers Development's about 24 percent. In contrast, companies providing waste-management and clean-up services and products did well and were the best bets for investors. For example, Midwesco Filter Resources (filter bags and accessories for air-pollution control systems) and Ionics (water purification equipment) both had a 1991–1992 stock price gain of over 40 percent. Groundwater Technology (consulting on soil and groundwater contamination) had a one-year gain of almost 15 percent, and TETRA Technologies (recycling and treatment services) had a gain of around 35 percent.

TRACKING CORPORATE SOCIAL BEHAVIOR

As pointed out in Chapter 4, there is no such thing as corporate sainthood and even the best of companies sometimes stub their toes socially. To aid investors in monitoring corporate social behavior, GOOD MONEY Publications began publication in 1992 of a "Social Investors' Watch List." The list consists of companies long known for corporate social responsibility but which had engaged in apparently questionable social practices. On the first list were:

Digital Equipment	Because of continuing losses, the company abandoned its no-involuntary-layoff policy in 1991. CEO Kenneth Olsen lost his cool in a press interview in 1992 when asked about possible further layoffs. He shouted to Boston-area reporters that it was none of anybody's business what happened inside the company—not shareholders, not employees, and not the general public. On July 19, 1992, Olsen abruptly resigned as president of DEC, 35 years after founding the company. Vice president Robert Palmer replaced Olsen, and it remained to be seen if Palmer could restore DEC's financial health and sense of corporate responsibility.
Corning, Inc.	Corning has one of the most aggressive affirmative action programs for women and minorities, especially African Americans. However, Corning owns 50 percent of Dow Corning and five of the company's representatives sit on DC's board. Corning also supplied the silicon for DC's implants. When the story broke about the possible health risks of the implants,

Corning's usually accessible CEO James Houghton was nowhere to be found by the press for comments on possible lapses and inadequacies in testing.

H. J. Heinz

This is another company known for community concern, especially on environmental issues, but CEO Anthony O'Reilly walked off with the highest 1991 executive paycheck—a whopping $75.1 million. During that year, Heinz's total sales fell about one percent, while net profit was off around 10 percent. The company provided no explanation for the discrepancy between O'Reilly's pay and corporate performance.

Johnson & Johnson

In 1992, a cancer expert charged that a J&J drug, Ergamisol, was being sold to veterinarians (to treat sheep for parasites) for $14, while the same drug was being sold to human patients (to treat colon cancer) for $1,250 to $1,500 for a year's supply. He stated that J&J had breached its commitment to set a moderate price for human use of the drug. J&J officials countered that the higher price reflected the necessary R&D expense to discover that a drug originally produced as a veterinarian product had a human use as well. The question was, who was right?

Procter & Gamble

P&G has been praised for having good employee practices, researching environmentally friendly products, and lessening its dependency upon animals for product testing. The company sells coffee in El Salvador. At the urging of Neighbor to Neighbor (NTN) with the help of the Interfaith Center for Corporate Responsibility, P&G agreed to take steps to protect the rights of small El Salvadoran coffee growers. NTN announced the lifting of an earlier boycott against P&G's products. However, the company was also threatened with a boycott by over 200 African American newspapers that charged the company with avoiding placing advertisements in minority newspapers.

Safety Kleen

By the early '90s, this company, once the favorite for all environmental portfolios, had accumulated enough environmental violations and penalties in California, Massachusetts, Texas, and Washington to convince U.S. Trust's Social Investment Committee that its stock would no longer be an appropriate holding.

In 1992, Progressive Asset Management, in cooperation with Kinder, Lydenberg, Domini & Company, began offering a "Social Research Service" for individuals and institutions. The service helps investors develop socially responsible investment policies, screens current investments, and monitors portfolio social and financial performance. The service either works with an investor's current investment manager, or, at the investor's request, suggests specialists in SRI.

SRI SPREADS GLOBALLY

One of the results of the new environmental concerns was the increasing realization by both corporations and investors that markets and economies in the world had become truly global. Social issues and problems now transcend national boundaries, and new strategies and practices, including SRI, are necessary. In 1991, Mitsuko Shimomura was appointed editor-in-chief of *Asahi Journal*, a highly respected Japanese weekly newsmagazine. She immediately organized a team consisting of reporters, a Tokyo International University professor, and graduate students to collect information from companies doing business in Japan, ranging from corporate disclosure information through family benefits to environmental awareness. The team consulted with members of the U.S. Council on Economic Priorities to develop research techniques. The result was an analysis of some seventy U.S. and Japanese companies ranked on eleven different social criteria. Among the best were Honda, IBM Japan, Matsushita, Sony, and Toyota. SRI was off and running in that country.

In 1992, *Business Week* magazine reported that Japanese companies were poised to become the world's leading suppliers of environmental-protection products and services. That country was far ahead of the U.S. in technologies and knowledge, since lax regulations and inexpensive fossil fuels in the U.S. provided little motivation for companies to change from business as usual. Tokyo Electric Power tested an electric car that ran as fast as 109 miles per hour and drove 340 miles at 25 miles per hour on one battery charge—both world records. Matsushita Electric Industrial Company was selling solar batteries worldwide. Hitachi Ltd. and Mitsubishi Heavy Industries Ltd. were selling everything from plant design to waste-water and air-pollution control.

Some U.S. companies had signed agreements with Japanese companies for joint ventures. Corning joined with Mitsubishi to use chemical catalysts to remove nitrogen-oxides from coal-fired power plants. Forster Wheeler Energy Corp. received a license from Ishikawajima-Harima Heavy Industries for the Japanese company's nitrogen-oxides removal technology for industrial and power plants. Zurn Industries joined with Ebara to build low-emission, industrial waste incinerators.

This transnational cooperation also has had other benefits. Japanese corporations have long used the *keiretsu* model—cooperation, rather than competition, between a consortium of suppliers, manufacturers, financial companies, and others critical in the overall conduct of a business. In the early 1990s, some U.S. companies discovered that this was not such a bad idea. In 1991, giant IBM stunned the U.S. financial community when it was announced that personal computers would be jointly marketed by IBM and its arch-rival Apple Computer. It appeared that cooperation would be more profitable to both companies than their trying to beat each other's brains out in the market place. General Motors suggested to the other U.S. automakers that it might be wise to reach an agreement not to produce so many duplicative models. Harley-Davidson abandoned the practice of dealing with dozens of suppliers, all of whom furiously competed with one another. Instead, H-D selected a fixed number of suppliers with whom they cooperated to improve their businesses, so that H-D would receive higher quality and lower-cost products.

In Europe, Vienna-based OKO-INVEST began publication of an environmental newsletter called *OKO-INVEST: Investment mit Verantwortung & Erfolg* (with responsibility and success). The newsletter tracks and reports on European companies, particularly Austrian, British, French, German, Hungarian, and Swiss firms. Plans were being made to report also on Czechoslovakian and Polish companies. In addition, the newsletter reports on U.S. companies from "a green perspective," such as IMCO Recycling. In Switzerland, Versicherungs Treuhand Zurich (Economical-Ecological Asset Management) offers a variety of services and funds, all designed to focus on environmental issues. Among the most innovative are Eco-Real Estate ("participation in Eco-high-tech buildings through real estate funds and Eco-mortgages"), Eco-Capital ("direct investment with an allotment of 90 percent in ecology"), and Eco-Life Insurance ("as much as is possible by life insurance law, premiums are invested in solar and other renewable energy projects").

All of the increasing global activity in SRI in recent years is evidence of a new consciousness, a consciousness summed up by the words of the Roman orator and statesman Marcus Tullius Cicero: "Socrates, indeed, when he was asked of what country he called himself, said 'Of the world'; for he considered himself an inhabitant and a citizen of the whole world."

EPILOGUE

Many people have become cynical and skeptical today for several reasons. First, as some recent research indicates, a large portion of the public believes that most people are merely out for themselves and that a for-profit economy fosters nothing but greed and avarice. Second, the world's social problems often seem so insurmountable and so severe that many people believe there is nothing that they as individuals can do. This cynicism and resignation obscure the fact that important change can be brought about even through the simplest of everyday economic acts. In addition to the options available through SRI, as individual *consumers* all of us can send powerful messages to companies about what we think is wrong or right about their business practices.

CAN CAPITALISM EVER BE ETHICAL?

In a major study, first published as a series of essays in 1904 and 1905, the German sociologist Max Weber raised the question of why capitalism first appeared and quickly flourished in Western culture. He argued that the single greatest influence was early

Puritanism and Protestantism. Early Protestant reformers maintained that proof of religious salvation could be found by living a kind of Puritan life in the here and now that proved salvation to themselves and others. That kind of life was characterized by hard work, thrift, frugality, saving, and reinvestment—what Weber called the Protestant work ethic.

These religious characteristics of work were especially compatible with early capitalism. Saving and reinvestment resulted in a growing economy. Though people saved because it was the "moral" thing to do and reflected the spirit of God, the reinvestment of these savings created more needed goods and services as well as new jobs. The concept of corporate social responsibility— the duty of for-profit corporations to respond to social issues— also goes back to the early English charters, by which merchants were given certain privileges with the understanding that companies would also serve the national and public interest.

During eighteenth-century capitalism, churches denounced excessive interest rates as usurious, as difficult as that may be for modern credit card holders to believe. Capitalist entrepreneurs wrote tracts about what constituted ethical economic practices. For example, it was considered unethical for one merchant to lure customers from another by artificially lowering prices or by similar inducements. Manipulation of prices was considered unethical since all merchants could not compete fairly. It was also seen as bad economically for a free market since prices should be determined by a free exchange between buyer and seller.

When capitalism moved from Europe to America, it became influenced by another quasi-religious philosophy known as millenarianism. Unlike European utopians, who saw the good life as far off in the future and dependent upon the controls of a strong central government, millenarians believed it was possible for free individuals to create paradise on earth in the here and now. One did not have to wait until after death to attain economic and social well-being. One model of the quintessential early capitalist was William Penn, who founded Pennsylvania in 1681. During his life he combined strong Quaker religious beliefs with political statesmanship and business acumen. It is no accident that Quakers have played a major role in the SRI movement.

Though the history of capitalism has had its share of robber barons, modern examples of capitalists who combine doing good with doing well are plentiful. In 1958 William and Vieve Gore founded W. L. Gore & Associates, a company that became famous for its Gore-Tex fabrics and fibers. The organization of this company was unlike anything taught in business schools. In a system of lattice organization, employees dealt directly with one another, one-on-one across both horizontal and vertical lines. The company had no titles, no orders, and no bosses. Reminiscent of the Mondragón cooperatives, commitment, rather than command, was the most important element. So alien was the concept of titles that one female associate, needing something for a business card, called herself "Supreme Commander," when Bill Gore told her she could use any title she wanted.

James W. Rouse also successfully combined business acumen with social responsibility. His real estate firm has refurbished city centers like Boston's Faneuil Marketplace, Philadelphia's Gallery at Market East, and Baltimore's Harborplace. In the 1960s Rouse became involved with the Church of the Saviour, a Washington, D.C., inner-city congregation interested in prison work, children's programs, and refugee problems in Thailand. In the 1970s members formed Jubilee Housing, Inc., to purchase and renovate run-down apartment buildings. Rouse borrowed $750,000 and bought two buildings. The day after Jubilee took control of the dilapidated tenements, the local government filed notice of more than nine hundred housing code violations. However, three years later all the violations had been removed with volunteer help. Rouse's real estate company also built the racially integrated town of Columbia, Maryland, at a time when an integrated community was considered dangerous social experimentation.

Historically the pursuit of profit does not have to result in unrestrained and destructive greed. What is needed is a new vision of how self-interest and collective interest can become mutually supportive. In their 1989 book *Healthy Pleasures* psychologist

Robert Ornstein and physician David Sobel question the commonly accepted notion that altruism and self-interest are always in conflict. They argue that medical research has disclosed that those who commit themselves to serve others, such as the Mother Teresas of the world, have lower blood pressure, lower feelings of distress and anxiety, better immune system functioning and live longer. As the authors put it, "The great surprise of human evolution may be that the highest form of selfishness is selflessness." This could be an appropriate battle cry for SRI.

MAKING A DIFFERENCE

Though this book is about investing, no book about SRI would be complete without mentioning socially responsible consuming (SRC). Consumer behavior is very much like investing. Consumers use money to accumulate assets for immediate or long-term use and, in some cases, long-term capital appreciation (the family house). Ever since Ralph Nader began forming his Public Interest Research Groups, SRC has been an important force in bringing about changes in the economy, and it is an important adjunct to SRI.

In 1986 SRC received a major boost with the publication of a study of 130 companies by the Council on Economic Priorities. The companies provided every imaginable product and service for ordinary consumers, from food through pharmaceuticals and household appliances and products to airline, hotel, and gasoline services. The authors of *Rating America's Corporate Conscience* ranked the companies in seven social categories, ranging from charitable contributions to nuclear weapons-related contracts. From this book consumers could learn that the makers of Progresso canned foods (Ogden Corporation), Whitman's candy (IC Industries), Sun Giant nuts (Tenneco), and Amana refrigerators (Raytheon) all were involved with weapons contracts. In contrast, the makers of Green Giant and LeSueur foods (Pillsbury), Godiva candy (Campbell Soup), and Fisher nuts (Beatrice Company) did not have weapons contracts.

To assist consumers in making social choices, the authors of CEP's study included, for some but not all product groupings, what they called "Authors' Company of Choice." This was not a recommendation to buy the listed products, nor did it necessarily have anything to do with product quality. It reflected the collective judgment of the authors of the study about what companies tended to be standouts after all the social information had been analyzed. The table on pages 176 and 177 illustrates how socially concerned consumers, using the CEP study, could identify product brand names of preferred versus less preferred companies in nine of the twelve product groupings in the study.

By mid-1990 socially concerned consumers could obtain a growing number of credit cards (known as affinity cards) that provided support for a variety of national environmental, political, and social action groups. These included cards issued by the Defenders of Wildlife, the Environmental Defense Fund, the National Wildlife Federation, the Sierra Club, and Working Assets. For each card issued and / or each use of the card a small donation is made to the organization. In the case of the Working Assets VISA card, donations have been made to such groups as the Africa Fund, Amnesty International, Greenpeace USA, the National Coalition for the Homeless, the National Gay and Lesbian Task Force, Oxfam America, and SANE.

Just as shareholder action can be an affective means for changing corporate practices, so can consumer boycotts and related public reaction. In 1989 the *Wall Street Journal* reported that when the Chrysler Corporation announced plans to close a plant in Kenosha, Wisconsin, the governor threatened a lawsuit, workers wore sweaters depicting Chrysler CEO Lee Iacocca with a Pinocchio-like nose, and consumers boycotted local Chrysler dealers. Iacocca, concerned about his image as a good guy, promised that all 1988 profits from Wisconsin operations would go to a fund to help unemployed workers and—ironically—hinted that the state might get some of the company's defense contract work.

By mid-1989 the Beech-Nut Nutrition Corporation was on the auction block to be sold by parent company Nestlé. The reason

| | Authors' Choices | |
PRODUCT GROUPS	COMPANY	BRAND NAMES
Bathroom tissues	Procter & Gamble	Banner, Charmin, White Cloud
Breads and baked goods	Campbell Soup	Pepperidge Farm
Canned beans	Quaker Oats	Van Camp's
Facial tissues	Scott Paper	Lady Scott, Scotties
Frozen meals	General Mills	Gorton's
Fruit/vegetable juices, drinks & mixes	Campbell Soup	Juice Works, Pepperidge Farm
Infant formula	Bristol Myers[2]	Enfamil, ProSobee
Soap	Procter & Gamble	Camay, Coast, Ivory, Safeguard, Zest
Typewriters	Xerox	Xerox

[1] Name changed in 1988 to Whitman Corporation.
[2] Merged with Squibb in 1989 to become Bristol-Myers Squibb.

was that consumers were boycotting the company. The big blow came when the public learned that the company's well-advertised apple juice for babies was nothing more than flavored water. Parents did not appreciate the fact that the company had been cheating on their children. Beech-Nut eventually paid about $9 million in fines and lawsuits, and its lasting image was of a company that had tried to con mothers and babies.

Both socially responsible investing and socially responsible consuming can make a big difference. For those who still despair that the social problems of the world are too great, take some solace in an old Chinese curse: "May you live in interesting times." However, for those who despair that time is running short for bringing about needed major changes in economic behavior, it is well to remember the words of the nineteenth-century German philosopher Arthur Schopenhauer: "There are three steps in the

Lower Ratings	
COMPANY	**BRAND NAMES**
James River	Marina, Nice 'n Soft, Northern, Vanity Fair
CPC International	Thomas' muffins
IC Industries[1]	B & M, Friend's
James River	Vanity Fair
ConAgra	Banquet, Classic Lite, Dinner Classics, Morton
Castle & Cooke	Dole
Abbott Labs	Similac, Isomil
American Brands	Aloe & Lanoiin, Fiesta, Jergens
Int'l. Bus. Machs.	IBM

revelation of any truth: in the first, it is ridiculed; in the second, resisted; in the third, it is considered self-evident." This book is dedicated to the belief that public awareness of the economic and social benefits of SRI is rapidly moving into that third phase.

APPENDICES

APPENDIX A

READINGS AND REFERENCES

This is not an exhaustive or complete listing of all possible references for ethically concerned businesspeople and investors. Rather, it is designed (1) to list the major references that were most important in the preparation of this book and (2) to provide examples of the kinds of references of most help and interest to concerned investors, by various topics and issues.

CONSUMER AND SHAREHOLDER ACTION

Council on Economic Priorities. *Shopping for a Better World*. New York: Ballantine Books, 1990.

Lydenberg, Steven, and staff of Council on Economic Priorities. *Rating America's Corporate Conscience*. Reading, Mass.: Addison-Wesley, 1986.

United Shareholders Association. *The Shareholder Proposal Process*. Undated.

Yepsin, Roger B., Jr., ed. *The Durability Factor: A Guide to Finding Long-lasting Cars, Housing, Clothing, Appliances, Tools and Toys*. Emmaus, Pa.: Rodale Press, 1982.

CORPORATE SOCIAL PROFILES AND CASE STUDIES

Close, Arthur C., and Gregory L. Bologna, eds. *National Directory of Corporate Public Affairs*, 2d ed. Washington, D.C.: Columbia Books, 1988.

Council on Economic Priorities. *Guide to Corporations: A Social Perspective.* Chicago: Swallow Press, 1974.

Ermann, M. David, and Richard J. Lundman. *Corporate and Governmental Deviance.* New York: Oxford University Press, 1987.

Inter-Hemispheric Education Resource Center. *The Central American Fact Book.* New York: Grove Press, 1986.

Kapstein, Jonathan, and John Hoerr, "Volvo's Radical New Plant: 'The Death of the Assembly Line?' " *Business Week* (August 28, 1989), 92–93.

Levering, Robert; Milton Moskowitz; and Michael Katz. *The 100 Best Companies to Work for in America.* Reading, Mass.: Addison-Wesley, 1984.

Moskowitz, Milton; Michael Katz; and Robert Levering. *Everybody's Business: An Almanac.* New York: Harper & Row, 1980.

———. *Everybody's Business: 1982 Update.* New York: Harper & Row, 1982.

———. *Everybody's Business Scoreboard: Corporate America's Winners, Losers and Also-Rans.* New York: Harper & Row, 1983.

Peters, Thomas J., and Robert H. Waterman, Jr. *In Search of Excellence: Lessons from America's Best-Run Companies.* New York: Harper & Row, 1982.

Whyte, William Foote, and Kathleen King Whyte. *Making Mondragon: The Growth and Dynamics of the Worker Cooperative Complex.* Ithaca, N.Y.: ILR Press, 1988.

Zeitz, Baila, and Lorraine Dusky. *The Best Companies for Women.* New York: Simon and Schuster, 1988 Pocket Books, 1989)

ETHICS AND MORALITY IN BUSINESS AND THE ECONOMY

Boulding, Kenneth E. *The Organizational Revolution: A Study in the Ethics of Economic Organization.* New York: Harper & Row, 1953.

Clinard, Marshall B., and Peter C. Yeager. *Corporate Crime.* New York: Free Press, 1980.

Deal, Terrence E., and Allan A. Kennedy. *Corporate Cultures: The Rites and Rituals of Corporate Life.* Reading, Mass.: Addison-Wesley, 1982.

Etzioni, Amitai. *The Moral Dimension: Toward a New Economics:* New York: Free Press, 1988.

Lenski, Gerhard. *The Religious Factor: A Sociological Study of Religion's Impact on Politics, Economics and Family Life.* New York: Doubleday, 1963.

May, Larry. *The Morality of Groups: Collective Responsibility, Group-Based Harm, and Corporate Rights.* South Bend, Ind.: University of Notre Dame Press, 1987.

Silk, Leonard, and David Vogel. *Ethics and Profits: The Crisis of Confidence in American Business.* New York: Simon and Schuster, 1976.

Sutherland, Edwin H. *White-Collar Crime.* New York: Dryden Press, 1949.

Walton, Clarence C. *Corporate Social Responsibilities.* Belmont, Calif.: Wadsworth, 1967.

————, ed. *The Ethics of Corporate Conduct.* Englewood Cliffs, N.J.: Prentice-Hall, 1977.

Weber, Max. *The Protestant Ethic and the Spirit of Capitalism,* tr. Talcott Parsons. New York: Charles Scribner's Sons, 1958.

HISTORIES, PHILOSOPHIES, AND SOCIAL THEORIES

Bruyn, Severyn T. *The Field of Social Investment.* Cambridge, England: Cambridge University Press, 1987.

Business Week team, *The Reindustrialization of America.* New York: McGraw-Hill, 1982.

Nisbet, Robert. *History of the Idea of Progress.* New York: Basic Books, 1980.

Roth, Guenther, and Claus Wittich, eds. *Max Weber: Economy and Society.* 2 vols. Berkeley: University of California Press, 1978.

Schumacher, E. F. *Small Is Beautiful: Economics as If People Mattered.* New York: Harper & Row Torchbooks, 1973.

Schumpeter, Joseph A. *Capitalism, Socialism and Democracy.* New York: Harper & Row, 1950.

HOW-TO STRATEGIES FOR BUSINESSPEOPLE AND INVESTORS

Council on Economic Priorities. *Pension Funds & Ethical Investment.* New York: Council on Economic Priorities, 1980.

Domini, Amy L., with Peter D. Kinder. *Ethical Investing.* Reading, Mass.: Addison-Wesley, 1984.

Ellman, Eugene. *The 1989 Canadian Guide to Profitable Ethical Investing.* Toronto, Canada: James Lorimer & Co., 1989.

Judd, Elizabeth. *Investing with a Social Conscience.* New York: Pharos Books, 1990.

Kilcullen, Michael. *Directory of Alternative Investments.* New York: Interfaith Center on Corporate Responsibility, 1985.

Lowry, Ritchie P. "Social Investing: Doing Good while Doing Well." *Futurist* (April 1982), 22–28.

Meeker-Lowry, Susan. *Economics as If the Earth Really Mattered.* Philadelphia: New Society Publishers, 1988.

Moore, Gary D. *The Thoughtful Christian's Guide to Investing.* Grand Rapids, Mich.: Zondervan Books, 1990.

Ouchi, William. *Theory Z.* Reading, Mass.: Addison-Wesley, 1981.

Rothchild, John. "Clean Money." *New England Monthly* (February 1986), 56–61.

Seibert, Donald V. *The Ethical Executive.* New York: Simon and Schuster, 1984.

Silverstein, Michael. *The Environmental Factor: Its Impact on the Future of the World Economy and Your Investments.* Chicago: Longman Financial Services Publishing, 1990.

―――, ed. *Directory of Environmental Investing.* 2d ed. Silver Spring, Md.: Business Publishers, 1990.

Simon, John G.; Charles W. Powers; and Jon P. Gunnemann. *The Ethical Investor: Universities and Corporate Responsibility.* New Haven, Conn.: Yale University Press, 1972.

Ward, Sue. *Socially Responsible Investment.* London, England: Ethical Investment Research Service and Directory of Social Change, 1986.

Warfield, Gerald. *How to Buy Foreign Stocks and Bonds.* New York: Harper & Row, 1985.

SPECIAL ISSUES AND PROBLEMS

Barnet, Richard J., and Ronald E. Muller. *Global Reach: The Power of the Multinational Corporations.* New York: Simon and Schuster, 1974.

Blasi, Joseph Raphael. *Employee Ownership: Revolution or Ripoff?* Cambridge, Mass.: Ballinger, 1988.

Ferrari, Paul L.; Jeffrey W. Kopf; and Raul L. Madrid. *U.S. Arms Exports: Policies and Contractors.* New York: Interfaith Center on Corporate Responsibility, 1987.

Hertsgaard, Mark. *Nuclear, Inc.: The Men and Money behind the Nuclear Industry.* New York: Pantheon Books, 1983.

Lernoux, Penny. *In Banks We Trust.* New York: Anchor Press / Doubleday, 1984.

Melman, Seymour. *Pentagon Capitalism: The Political Economy of War.* New York: McGraw-Hill, 1970.

―――. *The Permanent War Economy.* New York: Simon and Schuster, 1974.

Project on Military Procurement. *More Bucks, Less Bang: How the Pentagon*

Buys Ineffective Weapons. Washington, D.C.: Fund for Constitutional Government, 1983.

Rifkin, Jeremy, and Randy Barber. *The North Will Rise Again: Pensions, Politics and Power in the 1980s.* Boston: Beacon Press, 1978.

"Workers as Owners." *Labor Research Review,* no. 6 (Spring 1985). Published by Midwest Center for Labor Research, Chicago.

Appendix B

Information
Resources for SRI

This is not an extensive listing of all possible information resources for ethically and socially concerned businesspeople and investors. Rather, it is designed to list those principal resources that were utilized in the preparation of this book. Some of the organizations listed under "Information Specifically for Social Investors" (for example, ICCR and SIF) do publish and periodically update very complete listings for hundreds of different types of information and service resources available for ethical and social investors. Other organizations (such as Catalyst and GOOD MONEY Publications) have available complete listings of special resources (community-based funds and socially screened funds respectively). In addition, large-circulation newspapers (such as the *New York Times* and the *Wall Street Journal*) and magazines (such as *Business Week* and *Fortune*) are frequently excellent sources for tracking the social features, both bad and good, of corporations.

BANKS (WITH THE MOST EXTENSIVE SOCIAL SERVICES)

Community Capital Bank
Lyndon B. Comstock, Organizer
111 Livingston Street
Brooklyn, NY 11201
(718) 768-9344

Department of the Treasury
Fiscal Services
Bureau of Government Financial Operations
Washington, DC 20226
(Can provide a list of minority-owned banks and savings and loans)

Development Bank of Washington (In Organization)
2000 L Street NW, Suite 702
Washington, DC 20036
(202) 332-9333

National Federation of Community Development Credit Unions
(NFCDCU)
29 John Street, Room 903
New York, NY 10038
(212) 513-5191

Social Banking Programs, Inc.
14 Elliot Street
Brattleboro, VT 05301
(802) 257-0211

South Shore Bank
Seventy-first and Jeffery Boulevard
Chicago, IL 60649
(312) 288-1000, ext. 312, or (312) 288-7017

Vermont National Bank
Socially Responsible Banking Fund
P.O. Box 804
Brattleboro, VT 05301
(802) 257-7151 or (800) 544-7108

Women's World Banking
104 East Fortieth Street, Suite 607
New York, NY 10016
(212) 953-2390
(Promotes the worldwide entrepreneurship of women)

COMMUNITY-TARGETED PROGRAMS

Association for the Democratic Workplace (ADW)
1400 High Street
Eugene, OR 97401
(503) 638-8184
Newsletter: *Workplace Democracy*

E. F. Schumacher Society
Box 76, R.D. 3
Great Barrington, MA 01230
(413) 528-1737

Equity Trust
Chuck Matthei
RFD 1, Box 430
Voluntown, CT 06384
(203) 376-6174

Fund for Southern Communities:
552 Hill Street, SE
Atlanta, GA 30312
(404) 577-3178

Industrial Cooperative Association (ICA)
249 Elm Street
Somerville, MA 02114
(617) 628-7330

Institute for Community Economics, Inc. (ICE),
and National Association of Community Development Loan Funds
(NACDLF)
57 School Street
Springfield, MA 01105
(413) 746-8660
Newsletter: *Community Economics*

National Federation of Community Development Credit Unions
59 John Street, Eighth Floor
New York, NY 10038
(212) 513-7191 or (800) 437-8711

CORPORATIONS

Those wishing to contact corporations directly can find names of executives, headquarters' addresses, telephone numbers, and other information in *Standard & Poor's Register of Corporations* and *Value Line Investment Survey.* If you subscribe to or order these resources for your personal use, they are expensive. However, they can usually be found at a local library or in the library of a business school.

FINANCIAL MANAGEMENT AND SERVICES

Christian Brothers Investment Services, Inc.
245 Park Avenue, Tenth Floor
New York, NY 10167
(212) 272-6750 or (800) 592-8890
(For organizations listed in the *Official Catholic Directory*)

Clean Yield Asset Management
224 State Street
Portsmouth, NH 03801-9850
(603) 436-0820

First Affirmative Financial Network
410 North Twenty-First Street, No. 203
Colorado Springs, CO 80904
(719) 528-1343 or (800) 422-7284

Franklin Research and Development Corporation (FRDC)
711 Atlantic Avenue
Boston, MA 02111
(617) 423-6655
Newsletters: *Insight* and *Investing for a Better World*

    FRDC California Corporation
    65K Gate Five Road
    Sausalito, CA 94965
    (415) 332-5822

    FRDC—Northwest
    Market Place One, Suite 105
    2001 Western Avenue
    Seattle, WA 98121
    (206) 441-5855

Kinder, Lydenberg, Domini & Co., Inc.
7 Dana Street
Cambridge, MA 02138
(617) 547-7479

Progressive Asset Management
1814 Franklin Street, Suite 600
Oakland, CA 94612
(415) 834-3722 or (800) 527-8627
(Also offers an IRA designed to finance education,
research, and care to fight AIDS)

Smith Barney, Harris Upham & Company
Robert J. Schwartz
1345 Avenue of the Americas
New York, NY 10105
(212) 307-2407 or (800) 468-0019

The Social Responsibility Investment Group, Inc.
The Chandler Building, Suite 622
127 Peachtree Street, NE
Atlanta, GA 30303
(404) 577-3635

United States Trust Company (USTrust)
Dr. Robert B. Zevin and Stephen K. Moody
Asset Management Division—Trust Department
40 Court Street, Tenth Floor
Boston, MA 02108
(617) 726-7250

FOREIGN RESOURCES AND PUBLICATIONS

ARTUS Ethische Vermögensverwaltung GmbH
Beethovenplatz 1
D-5300 Bonn 1
Germany
Phone: 0228 / 65112

Der Newsletter des Wertewandels
Christopher Pfluger
Viaduktstrasse 8
CH-4512 Bellach
Switzerland
Phone: 065 / 38-25-25
Newsletter: *Die Neue Wirtschaft*

Ethical Growth Fund
Box 24807, Postal Station C
Vancouver, British Columbia V5T 4E9
Canada

Ethical Investment Research Service (EIRIS)
4.01 Bondway Business Centre
71 Bondway
London SW8 15Q
England
Phone: (01) 735-1351
Newsletter: *Ethical Investor*

Eugene Ellmen
138 Cambridge Avenue
Toronto, Ontario M4K 2L8
Canada
Phone: (416) 466-3860
Newsletter: *Conscientious Investor*

GLS Gemeinschaftsbank eG
Oskar-Hoffman-Strasse 25
4630 Bochum 1
Germany
                and

Haussmannstrasse 50
7000 Stuttgart 1
Germany

Institut de la Communication Sociale
26 Boulevard Raspail
75007 Paris
France
Phone: (1) 45-48-81-73

Louis Deschamps
37 Avenue Duquesne
75007 Paris
France
Phone: (1) 45-55-11-24

Max Deml
Green Club
Parliament
A-1017 Vienna
Austria
Phone: 43 / 1 / 40110 / 538
            and
Lindengasse 43 / 17
A-1070 Vienna
Austria

MoneyMatters Financial Group Pty. Limited
Suite 3, 4–8 Waters Road
Neutral Bay 2089, New South Wales
Australia
Phone: (02) 953-0599

North Coast Ethical Credit Union
Freepost No. 60, P.O. Box 402
Lismore 2480, New South Wales
Australia
Phone: (066) 221-511

Occidental Environmental Opportunities Fund
Occidental Centre, 601 Pacific Highway
St. Leonards 2065, New South Wales
Australia
Phone: (02) 957-0957
(Owned by Occidental Life Insurance Company of Australia)

Pensions & Investment Research Consultants (PIRC)
40 Bowling Green Lane
London ECIR ONE
England
Phone: 01-833-4432

Research and Information Service in Ethical Investment
Vincent Commenne
Rue de Beauvechain 37
B-5991 Tourinnes-la-Grosse
Belgium
Phone: 32-10-86-01-38

The Social Investment Organization
447-366 Adelaide Street East
Toronto, Ontario M5A 3K9
Canada
(416) 360-6047
Newsletter: *SIO Forum*

Taskforce on the Churches and Corporate Responsibility
129 St. Clair Avenue West
Toronto, Ontario M4V 1N5
Canada
Phone: (416) 923-1758
Newsletter: *Monthly Mailing*

YWCA Ethical Investment Trust
Global Funds Management (Vic) Ltd.
Freepost No. 190, 99 Mount Street
North Sydney 2060, New South Wales
Australia
Phone: (02) 957-5820

GENERAL AND SPECIAL INFORMATION

American Association of Individual Investors
625 North Michigan Avenue
Chicago, IL 60611
(312) 280-0170
Newsletter: *AAII Journal*

Center for Defense Information
1500 Massachusetts Avenue, NW
Washington, DC 20005
(202) 862-0700
Newsletter: *Defense Monitor*

Department of Economics
Box 14
Mankato State University
Mankato, MN 56001
Newsletter: *Human Economy Newsletter*

Federation of American Scientists
307 Massachusetts Avenue, NE
Washington, DC 20002
(202) 546-3300
Newsletter: FAS *Public Interest Report*

Intermediate Technology Development Group
of North America, Inc.
The Bootstrap Press
777 United Nations Plaza, Suite 9A
New York, NY 10017
(212) 953-6920

South-North News Service
4 West Wheelock Street
Hanover, NH 03755
(603) 643-5071
Newsletter: *Third World Week*

Union of Concerned Scientists
26 Church Street
Cambridge, MA 02238
(617) 547-5552
Newsletter: *Nucleus*

United Shareholders Association
1667 K Street, NW, Suite 770
Washington, DC 20006
(202) 393-4600
Newsletter: USA *Advocate*

INFORMATION SPECIFICALLY FOR SOCIAL INVESTORS

The Africa Fund
198 Broadway
New York, NY 10038
(212) 962-1210

Bay Area Socially Responsible Investment Professionals
% The Parnassus Fund
244 California Street, Suite 210
San Francisco, CA 94111
(415) 362-3505

Catalyst, Inc.
P.O. Box 1308
Montpelier, VT 05602

(802) 233-7943
Newsletter: *Catalyst: Economics for the Living Earth*

Clean Yield Publications, Ltd.
Box 1880
Greensboro, VT 05842
(802) 533-7178
Newsletter: *Clean Yield*

Co-op America
2100 M Street, NW, Suite 310
Washington, DC 20036
(202) 872-5307 or (800) 424-COOP
Newsletter: *Building Economic Alternatives*

Council on Economic Priorities (CEP)
30 Irving Place
New York, NY 10003
(212) 420-1133
Newsletter: *CEP Newsletter*

Data Center
464 Nineteenth Street
Oakland, CA 94612
(415) 835-4692

GOOD MONEY Publications, Inc.
Box 363
Worcester, VT 05682
(802) 223-3911 or (800) 535-3551
Newsletters: *GOOD MONEY* and *NETBACK*

INFACT
256 Hanover Street
Boston, MA 02113
(617) 742-4583

Interfaith Center on Corporate Responsibility (ICCR)
475 Riverside Drive, Room 566
New York, NY 10115
(212) 870-2936
Newsletter: *Corporate Examiner*

Investor Responsibility Research Center (IRRC)
1755 Massachusetts Avenue, NW, Suite 600
Washington, DC 20036
(202) 234-7500
Newsletter: *News for Investors*

Management Reports, Inc.
101 West Union Wharf

Boston, MA 02109
Journal: *Business and Society Review*

Mavis Publications, Inc.
1107 Hazeltine Boulevard, Suite 530
Chaska, MN 55318
(612) 448-8864
Magazine: *Business Ethics*

National Center for Employee Ownership (NCEO)
2201 Broadway, Suite 807
Oakland, CA 94612
(415) 272-9461
Newsletter: *Employee Ownership Report*

National Wildlife Federation
1400 Sixteenth Street
Washington, DC 20036
(800) 432-6564
(Tracks major polluters)

New Consumer Institute
700 North Milwaukee Avenue, Suite 204
Vernon Hills, IL 60061
(708) 816-0306
Newsletter: *Conscious Consumer*

New England Business Association for Social Responsibility
(NEBASR)
David L. Conti
Longfellow Tennis & Fitness
524 Boston Post Road
Wayland, MA 01778
(617) 890-4542
Newsletter: *Corporate Citizen*

New Options, Inc.
Mark Satin
2005 Massachusetts Avenue, NW, lower level
Washington, DC 20036
(202) 822-0929
Newsletter: *New Options*

Nuclear Free America
325 East Twenty-fifth Street
Baltimore, MD 21218
(301) 235-3575
(Tracks weapons contractors)

Nuclear Information and Resource Service
1616 P Street, NW, Suite 160

Washington, DC 20036
(202) 328-0002
Newsletter: *Nuclear Monitor*

Program in Social Economy and Social Justice
Department of Sociology
Boston College
Chestnut Hill, MA 02167
(617) 552-4130
Newsletter: *Social Report*

Social Investment Forum (SIF)
430 First Avenue North, No. 290
Minneapolis, MN 55401
(612) 333-8338
Newsletter: *FORUM*

SOCIALLY SCREENED FUNDS*

	TYPE OF FUND	DEPOSIT REQUIREMENTS (INITIAL / SUBSEQUENT)
Amana Mutual Funds Trust 429 North Pennsylvania Street Indianapolis, IN 46204	Islamic mutual fund	$100 / $25
Calvert-Ariel Growth Fund 1700 Pennsylvania Avenue, NW Washington, DC 20006 (301) 951-4820 or (800) 368-2748	Aggressive growth mutual fund	$2,000 / $250
Calvert Social Investment Fund 1700 Pennsylvania Avenue, NW Washington, DC 20006 (301) 951-4820 or (800) 368-2748	Bond, equity money market, and mutual funds	$1,000 / $250 (for all 4 funds)

(Members of the Union of Concerned Scientists can invest in this fund and have the sales fee donated to UCS in the name of the sponsor.)

	TYPE OF FUND	DEPOSIT REQUIREMENTS (INITIAL / SUBSEQUENT)
Catholic Income Trust Alpine Mutual Fund Trust 650 South Cherry Street, Suite 700 Denver, CO 80222 (303) 321-2211 or (800) 826-6677	Catholic bonds fund	$1,000 / $250
Catholic United Investment Trust Christian Brothers Investment Services, Inc. (CBIS) 245 Park Avenue New York, NY 10167 (212) 272-6750 or (800) 592-8890	Balanced fund	$25,000

	TYPE OF FUND	DEPOSIT REQUIREMENTS (INITIAL / SUBSEQUENT)
Common Fund 363 Reef Road, P.O. Box 940 Fairfield, CT 06431 (203) 254-1211	South Africa-free balanced, bond and equity funds	$50,000
Dreyfus Third Century Fund Dreyfus Service Corporation EAB Plaza East Tower Uniondale, NY 11556 (800) 782-6620	Mutual fund	$2,000 / $100
Merrill Lynch Eco-Logical Trust 1990 Unit Investment Trusts P.O. Box 9015 Princeton, NJ 08503 (609) 282-8721	Ecological mutual fund	100 units minimum at current price ($1,046 on 6/29/90)
Miller, Anderson & Sherred One Tower Bridge West Conshohoken, PA 19428 (215) 940-5000	Choice of five portfolios	$1,000,000 / $1,000
New Alternatives Fund 295 Northern Boulevard Great Neck, NY 11021 (516) 466-0808	Environmental mutual fund	$2,650 / $500
Parnassus Fund 244 California Street, Suite 210 San Francisco, CA 94111 (415) 362-3505	Contrarian mutual fund	$2,000 / $100
Pax World Fund 224 State Street Portsmouth, NH 03801 (603) 431-8022	Antiwar mutual fund	$250 / $50
Schield: Progressive Environmental Fund Schield Securities, Inc. 300 Union Boulevard, Suite 410 Denver, CO 80228 (303) 985-9999 or (800) 826-8154	Ecological mutual fund	$1,000 / $100
Working Assets Money Fund 230 California Street San Francisco, CA 94111 (415) 989-3200 or (800) 533-3863	Money market fund	$1,000 / $100

(Also offers a VISA card and long-distance Sprint telephone service, both of which provide annual donations to civil rights, environmental, peace and other activist groups.)

*Ones in the United States with the most extensive and reliable social screens. For some of the foreign funds mentioned in this book, see "Foreign Resources and Publications" in this appendix.

APPENDIX C

GLOSSARY OF COMMON INVESTMENT TERMS

SHORT DEFINITIONS FOR FIFTY-THREE INVESTMENT TERMS USED IN THIS BOOK

An excellent reference is the 699-page *The Money Encyclopedia: The Comprehensive Resource of Information on Personal Finance, Business Practices, and the Worldwide Economic System*, edited by Harvey Rachlin (New York: Harper & Row, 1984).

AMERICAN DEPOSITORY RECEIPTS—Securities traded on the U.S. stock exchanges and representing ownership of foreign stocks.

AMERICAN STOCK EXCHANGE (ASE)—An aggressive competitor of the Big Board. Lists the securities of companies that cannot meet the NYSE's capitalization or other listing requirements or companies that think they have higher visibility by being listed on this exchange because it has far fewer listings than the NYSE. Some companies list their stocks on the NYSE and other securities (such as bonds) on the ASE.

ASSETS—Possessions having present or future economic value to the owner (cash, property, etc.)

BANKRUPTCY—A legal determination that an individual or a corporation is unable to pay debts. The law allows a period of time in order to pay creditors by reorganizing financial and business affairs under court direction.

BEAR MARKET—A period of time during which security prices follow a downward trend.

BETA—A measure of a stock's volatility. A beta of 1.00 means that the stock moves up and down in one-to-one relationship with the market as a whole.

A beta of greater than 1.00 (say, 1.20) means that the stock moves up or down more as the market also moves up or down, while a beta of less than 1.00 (say, 0.85) means the stock moves up or down less than the market. A beta of 0 (highly unusual) means that the stock moves contrary to market trends. For example, by late-summer 1990 the fifteen stocks on GOOD MONEY's Utility Average had an average beta of 0.74 compared with a beta of 0.80 for the DJUA stocks. This reflected the fact that the GMUA had been falling less in value than the DJUA in the generally downward markets at that time.

BIG BOARD—The New York Stock Exchange

BOND FUND—Funds in which individuals' investments are pooled and the combined total is used by a professional manager to invest in high-yielding corporate, municipal, and governmental bonds.

BOOK VALUE—A corporation's net worth measured by all assets less liabilities. The resulting amount is divided by the number of common stock shares outstanding to express book value per share.

BROKER—One who is a middle person between buyers and sellers, unlike a dealer, who buys and sells her or his own account.

BULL MARKET—A period of time during which security prices follow an upward trend.

CALL—See: OPTIONS.

CAPITALIZATION—The market worth of a corporation determined by multiplying the value of a share of common stock by the number of shares outstanding.

CERTIFICATES OF DEPOSIT (CDs)—Short-term money market instruments issued by banks and carrying a fixed interest rate to a set maturity date.

COMMON STOCKS—Securities representing an ownership interest in a company.

CONTRARIAN FUNDS—Funds whose professional manager uses a contrarian philosophy by investing in the securities of currently out-of-favor companies. A contrarian may buy when everyone else is selling and sell when everyone else is buying.

CO-OP—A form of ownership where a buyer purchases shares in a corporation, partnership, or trust and shares proportionately with other owners in the assets and liabilities of the common ownership. A cooperative ownership may not be individually transferred or sold.

CREDIT UNION—A not-for-profit cooperative financial institution that is owned and collectively controlled by its members.

DOW JONES STOCK AVERAGES—Statistical indicators of broad stock price fluctuations in the stock markets published by Dow Jones & Company. The Dow Jones Industrial Average (DJIA) was started in 1896 and is the oldest continuous stock price average in the United States. It consists of the stocks of thirty major industrial companies that trade on the NYSE and are held by many individual and institutional investors. The Dow Jones Utility Average (DJUA) consists of the stocks of fifteen public utilities that trade on the NYSE.

ESOP—An employee stock ownership plan whereby employees can purchase shares of stock in the company for which they work, either by cash payments or by withholding a portion of their pay.

FORTUNE 500 and 1,000—*Fortune* magazine listings of the five hundred and one thousand largest companies in the United States. Used to track corporate performance in such areas as assets, sales, profits, market value, and earnings per share of stock. *Fortune* also publishes special 500s for particular industries such as the *Fortune* Industrials 500 and the *Fortune* Service 500.

FUNDAMENTAL ANALYSIS—Evaluating investments on the basis of the relationship between the current price of a corporation's securities and such factors as the company's future earnings, condition of the economy, industry trends, and competence of the company's management to deal with employees, technological innovations, and the like.

FUTURES—Contracts for future delivery of securities (or commodities) at a set price and at a specified time. Highly speculative, since guesses are being made that the future price will go up or down and relatively little initial margin deposit is required.

GOOD MONEY STOCK AVERAGES—Statistical indicators of broad stock price fluctuations in the stock markets published by GOOD MONEY Publications, Inc. The GOOD MONEY Industrial Average (GMIA) consists of the stocks of thirty industrial companies that have good and responsible records for a variety of social issues. The GOOD MONEY Utility Average (GMUA) consists of the stocks of fifteen public utilities with good and responsible records for pollution control, development of alternative and renewable energy sources, energy conservation, and cogeneration. Most of the stocks on both the GMIA and GMUA come from the NYSE, though stocks of companies trading on the ASE and NASDAQ market are used when positive social features warrant inclusion on the averages. The securities of some foreign companies have also appeared on the GMIA when traded as ADRs on the NYSE. The performances of the GMIA and GMUA have been compared with the performances of the DJIA and DJUA since the end of 1976 in order to determine the impact of making ethical and social judgments upon financial return, for both investors and businesses.

GOVERNMENT AGENCY SECURITIES—Bonds and notes sold by agencies of a government.

GROSS NATIONAL PRODUCT (GNP)—The market value of the goods and services produced in a nation. Some critics argue that the GNP is not a very good measure of a country's wealth because so many things are excluded (for example, purely financial transactions, trading in secondhand items, housework, child rearing, etc.).

INDIVIDUAL RETIREMENT ACCOUNT (IRA)—A tax-deferred investment plan that permits a wage earner (and spouse) to save a portion of income for retirement or legally to shelter income from current taxation.

LAND TRUST—See: TRUST.

LEVERAGING—Magnifying rates of return by investing with borrowed funds. Excessive leveraging is considered risky because it substantially increases debt.

LIABILITY—Any actual or potential financial obligation.

LIQUIDATION—The sale of an asset or the closing out of a company, pension plan, or other investment.

LIQUIDITY—The ability to turn assets into cash rapidly without penalty.

MARGIN—The amount of an investor's deposit expressed as a percentage of the market value of the investment. A low margin can signal high risk.

MARKET—Economic transactions related by geography and / or the types of transactions, or the opportunity to engage in economic transactions.

MONEY MARKET FUNDS—Funds in which individuals' investments are pooled and the combined total is used by a professional manager to invest in high-yield, short-term money market instruments, such as CDs, corporate bonds, and government agency securities.

MUTUAL FUNDS—Funds in which individuals' investments are pooled and the combined total is used by a professional manager to invest in a variety of instruments, primarily common stocks.

NASDAQ MARKET (NATIONAL ASSOCIATION OF SECURITIES DEALERS AUTOMATED QUOTATIONS)—A computerized system for storing and transmitting price quotations for securities. Also see: OVER-THE-COUNTER MARKET.

NET ASSET VALUE—Total assets less total liabilities divided by number of shares outstanding.

NEW YORK STOCK EXCHANGE (NYSE)—The major market in the United States that lists the securities of major corporations with high capitalization.

OPTIONS—Rights to buy (call) or sell (put) a fixed amount of stock at a specified price within a particular period of time. More speculative than ordinary stock buying and selling since guesses are being made about whether or not the stock's price will go up or down within the specified period of time.

OVER-THE-COUNTER MARKET (OTC)—The largest securities market in the United States. Includes all new equity issues offered to the public for the first time, the securities quoted on the NASDAQ, common stocks less actively traded and not quoted on the NASDAQ, and exchange-listed securities traded off the floors of the exchanges. All these securities number in the tens of thousands.

PAR VALUE—The nominal or face value of a security. The par value is usually much lower than the security's market value.

P / E RATIO—A measure of the price of a share of stock to earnings per share of stock, designed to show whether or not a stock's price is reasonable. P / Es around 11 or 12 are considered a conservative investment. P / Es over 20 are considered to reflect greater risk.

PINK SHEET—A listing of the securities of small companies, not listed on the three major exchanges, that have a relatively low trading volume and little liquidity.

PORTFOLIO—An assortment and collection of investments.

PUT—See: OPTIONS.

REVOLVING LOAN FUND—Funds granting "open-end" credit that can be used at the borrower's discretion up to a prescribed limit.

RISK—The probability of loss and the extent of potential loss.

S&P 500—A stock price index started by Standard & Poor's Corporation in 1917. Consists of four hundred industrials, forty public utilities, twenty transportations, and forty financial companies. The stocks come mostly from the NYSE, though the stocks of some large companies that trade on the ASE are included. The index is market value-weighted rather than price-weighted (as are the Dow Jones and GOOD MONEY averages). Each stock on the S&P 500 is multiplied by the number of shares of stock outstanding in order to compute the value of the S&P 500 Index. Standard & Poor's also publishes an S&P 1000.

SECURITIES—Investment instruments (stocks, bonds, etc.) issued by companies and agencies in order to raise money.

SPECULATION—Investing that involves a high degree of risk because the judgment about future profitability is highly subjective and conjectural (based on little existing evidence) and the investment is subject to chance factors. Much speculation is no different from gambling.

STOCK INDEX—An artificially constructed average of stocks used to measure the performance of the stock market as a whole or to reflect the performance of various types of industry groups.

STOCK INDEX OPTIONS AND FUTURES—Options and futures on stock indexes, rather than on individual stocks. See: OPTIONS and FUTURES.

TECHNICAL ANALYSIS—Evaluating investments on the basis of the assumption that future prices of securities can be predicated by analyzing the past performance of the stock market as a whole. Technicians are sometimes called chartists since they develop detailed charts of historic stock price performance that identify market tops, bottoms, cycles, and upward and downward trends.

TRUST—An entity created and financed by one person (or group of people), usually for the benefit of other people, and controlled by a trustee. Trusts can involve all types of investments (stocks, bonds, land, etc.).

VALUE LINE, INC.—An independent investment adviser registered under the Investment Advisers Act of 1940 and publishers of advisory surveys and reports.

YIELD—Interest or dividends expressed as a percentage of the current market value of the investment. Compounded yield is the higher percentage if the interest or dividends are allowed to remain on deposit and accumulate their own yield as part of the total principal.

APPENDIX D

RELATIVE
PERFORMANCE
MEASURES

RELATIVE PERFORMANCE OF THE GMIA AND GMUA COMPARED WITH THE DJIA AND DJUA FROM THE END OF 1976 THROUGH 1989

Most individual investors and the popular press use absolute measures of performance since they are interested in whether or not investments have had actual gains or losses over time. In contrast, institutional investors are interested in how their portfolios have performed in comparison with the market as a whole or in comparison with market averages or other portfolios. As a result, they often use relative measures of performance. A measure of relative strength is calculated by dividing the value of the portfolio or stock group by the measure of the market as a whole.

The relative strength of the two GOOD MONEY averages compared with the Dow Jones averages can be calculated by dividing the former by the latter for specific periods of time. The results of this calculation are as shown on the next page.

| END OF | GMIA/DJIA | | GMUA/DJUA | |
	RELATIVE MEASURE	ANNUAL CHANGE	RELATIVE MEASURE	ANNUAL CHANGE
1976	.0276	—	.2112	—
1977	.0363	+31.5%	.2276	+7.8%
1978	.0418	+15.2	.2183	−4.1
1979	.0482	+15.3	.2098	−3.9
1980	.0518	+5.4	.2050	−2.3
1981	.0661	+30.1	.2281	+11.3
1982	.0639	−3.3	.2889	+26.3
1983	.0701	+9.7	.3440	+19.1
1984	.0694	−1.0	.2911	−15.4
1985	.0826	+19.0	.2960	+1.7
1986	.0726	−12.1	.3494	+18.0
1987	.0743	+2.3	.3624	+3.7
1988	.0746	+.4	.3643	+5.3
1989	.0752	+.8	.3171	−13.0
	Annual Average: +8.7%		*+4.2%*	

Relative measures reflect the percentage of change, rather than arithmetic change. The result can be plotted on a semilog graph to depict the change visually. As the accompanying graph indicates, the GMIA changed in an upward direction far more rapidly than the DJIA in seven of the thirteen years and slightly more rapidly in an upward direction in three of the years. The GMUA changed in an upward direction far more rapidly than the DJUA in six of the years, and slightly more rapidly in an upward direction in two of the years.

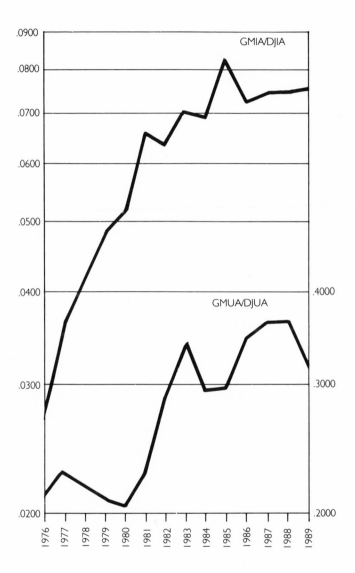

INDEX OF COMPANIES AND ORGANIZATIONS

Bond, equity, mutual and money market funds are listed in the Index of Subjects under the name of the fund.

INDEX OF SUBJECTS

Also refer to the Table of Contents for major subjects and topics.